PRAISE FOR **THE TODD GLASS SITUATION**

"A brilliant and very original comedian. . . . There are plenty of laughs. . . . Yet his account of his lifelong struggle to be honest about his sexuality is also serious, sad and ultimately triumphant."

—*The New York Times Book Review*

"Comedian Todd Glass has written a brave, amusing book about the hardest challenge of his life: Coming out. . . . How he does this and how it goes are some of the most brave writing I've read of late . . . by turns funny and frank and often both."

—Blogcritics

"A reliably funny and entertaining memoir . . . Glass' engaging delivery reflects his honest quest to live openly and abandon his early embarrassment about his sexuality. This memoir will appeal to Glass' fan base, as well as readers looking for stories of self-acceptance and triumph over shame."

—*Publishers Weekly*

"Glass clearly seeks to entertain with this comic picaresque, yet like his idol George Carlin, he also seeks to tell the truth, which he does with compassion and empathy throughout. A humorous, lively and humane memoir."

—*Kirkus Reviews*

"Unlike most memoirs by comedians, [Glass] actually addresses an important social issue. . . . While the chapters about his career are fun and interesting, it's the chapters about acknowledging his own truth and helping others to address theirs that makes this a great book to read and discuss with others."

D1458029

THE
TODD
GLASS
SITUATION

A Bunch of Lies About My Personal Life and a Bunch of True Stories About My 30-Year Career in Stand-Up Comedy

TODD GLASS
with JONATHAN GROTENSTEIN

SIMON & SCHUSTER PAPERBACKS

New York   London   Toronto   Sydney   New Delhi

Simon & Schuster Paperbacks
An Imprint of Simon & Schuster, Inc.
1230 Avenue of the Americas
New York, NY 10020

First Simon & Schuster trade paperback edition June 2015

SIMON & SCHUSTER PAPERBACKS and colophon are registered
trademarks of Simon & Schuster, Inc.

For information about special discounts for bulk purchases, please contact Simon
& Schuster Special Sales at 1-866-506-1949 or business@simonandschuster.com.

The Simon & Schuster Speakers Bureau can bring authors to your live event. For
more information or to book an event, contact the Simon & Schuster Speakers
Bureau at 1-866-248-3049 or visit our website at www.simonspeakers.com.

Interior design by Ruth Lee-Mui
Jacket design by Michael Accordino
Jacket photography by Robert Sebree

Manufactured in the United States of America

10   9   8   7   6   5   4   3   2   1

The Library of Congress has cataloged the hardcover edition as follows:

Glass, Todd.
   The Todd Glass situation : a bunch of lies about my personal life and a bunch
of true stories about my 30-year career in stand-up comedy / Todd Glass with
Jonathan Grotenstein.
      pages cm
1. Glass, Todd. 2. Comedians—United States—Biography. I. Grotenstein,
Jonathan. II. Title.
   PN2287.G5535A3 2014
   792.7'6028092—dc23
                                        2013042084

ISBN 978-1-4767-1441-7
ISBN 978-1-4767-1446-2 (pbk)
ISBN 978-1-4767-1450-9 (ebook)

CONTENTS

CONTENTS

CONTENTS

THE TODD GLASS SITUATION

PREFACE

by Marc Maron

You think you know a guy.

I have known Todd Glass for about twenty-five years, half my life. We were never that close, but I always knew him, kinda. We are in the same business. We all know Todd. I knew Todd was hilarious, big-hearted, persistent, incredibly quick-witted, original, and absolutely one of the most fun people in the world to be around.

I had no idea he was gay. None.

I never thought about it, never once. I say "gay" because I know Todd has a hard time saying that word, using it, in relation to himself or others. It's a label. It implies something. People make assumptions and attach stereotypes to the idea of gayness. I respect Todd's discomfort with the word "gay." Which is why I'm using it a lot. Gay. Todd is gay. So what? Todd was Todd. I think Todd thinks that too. That's why he didn't think it was necessary for anyone to know he's gay. Todd is Todd. He actually couldn't be any more Todd. Especially now that I know he's gay.

I'm a comic. I host a podcast. Lots of people listen to it. My guests are mostly comedians. It is my belief that comics can talk about anything. Our job is to sit around and think about stuff so there is very little we can't speak to or about. We embrace even the most difficult parts of life. We filter the world into funny. We have risked it all to do what we do, and there's an amazing freedom in that. We don't live by the same rules as everyone else. We can be brutally honest because we're funny. It's our job.

Todd called me one night. He left a message that he needed to talk to me. It sounded urgent. I had never talked to Todd on the phone in my life, but he needed help. My help. I called him back. He was a little more intense than usual but funny as always. If I recall correctly he was calling from his parents' house. I asked him what was up. He didn't sound sad or scared. He sounded a little fed up with himself and excited. He had resolve. He told me he wanted to come out and he wanted to do it on my show. He sounded like he had been wrestling with the decision to do it for a long time.

Todd chose my show because he knew that comics listened to it. He also knew that people who like to listen to people talk about the struggle of being a person listen to it. Todd wanted to come out, but he only wanted to do it once. He wanted word to travel, as opposed to e-mailing everyone he knew with the subject line "Hey, I'm gay. Just kidding. No, really, I am. What?" My show would enable him to do that.

When he told me I was surprised but I wasn't that surprised. You know when you know someone, even casually, and there's just a missing piece and when you hear it or see it, you get it? "Of course, that makes sense. How could I not have known?" Well, because it shouldn't matter.

My first thought after he told me was, "Am I the right guy

to do this?" As if it was a job that someone could handle more efficiently than me. "Isn't there a guy who does that, professionally?" I was happy that he was going to do it for his sake, but I had my own insecurities. I wanted it to be a good experience for him. I wanted to be there in any way I could to help him out with it. I didn't want to make it about me and I wanted to be a good sounding board for this big event in his life. I told him I would be honored to be there for him. He said he didn't know when it would happen but it would happen soon. He had to take care of some things. I said okay.

He would call me every other week or so for a month or two telling me that it was still happening. He would tell me with a tone like I was pressuring him. I wasn't. I think knowing he made the commitment to me to do it on the show forced him to pressure himself. I had my own preparation to do. I had to make myself understand that I was just there to support Todd and listen to him and push him when he needed a push and reel him in when he started to get away from the feelings. I was very conscious of my role.

When we finally sat down in my garage to record the show, Todd had really gotten himself into a mental place where he could do it. I can't imagine the adrenaline and intensity of saying something that will change your life forever, something that you had not been able to say for your entire life. Something so honest, revealing, and precise that it could be the key to your freedom, but also so frightening that you could not utter it before. It was an exciting day. Todd handled it with humor, candor, and humility. It was an amazing conversation. It reverberated.

I don't think what kept Todd from coming out was shame, specifically. He just thought he was protecting himself. I think

Todd is very comfortable being gay. I think that the energy it took to manage the secret had defined his entire life to the point where it had become second nature, and that became draining. I think what drove him to come out was anger. Anger at the secret, anger at himself, and anger that we live in a culture where the hostility or judgment you think will come at you for being who you are corners you into hiding yourself. So I guess it was shame. Todd called bullshit on himself, finally. What drove him to do it above anything else were kids who are bullied, shunned, beat up, and killed for being who they are. I think if there was any kind of shame that drove Todd, it was the shame of not standing up for himself or those kids.

Todd is now a real stand-up guy.

The feedback from the show was amazing. E-mails came in telling stories of gratitude for the strength and honesty Todd put out into the world. It helped people. It gave people strength. It made people feel less alone. It made it okay.

Todd calls me every few months to tell me he's still gay.

THE CORONET
(PART ONE)

Todd's act develops an unexpected wrinkle.

I'm standing backstage at Largo at the Coronet where, once every few months, Sarah Silverman invites a group of comedians to put on a show. Tonight's lineup includes Sarah, Jeff Ross, and Chelsea Peretti. I'm the closing act. I can't wait to get out there.

I've been a stand-up comedian for almost thirty years and I can honestly tell you, without exaggeration, that it is my favorite thing to do. Every time I'm about to take the stage I feel like a kid twenty feet from the entrance to Disneyland. Performing gives me an adrenaline rush like no other. Some nights I'm so amped I'll sprint from backstage right into the middle of the crowd, doing some silly bit as I run up and down the aisles.

Tonight is one of those nights. Sarah introduces me and

I go straight for the crowd, overenthusiastically greeting each and every member of the audience, an exaggerated take on a comic who's way too eager to please.

Five minutes later, when I finally make my way to the stage, I feel light-headed. My heart is pounding too fast and I can't catch my breath. So I turn it into a joke:

"Hey, what if I was having a heart attack and you guys didn't believe me?"

A few laughs.

"No, really . . . I'm having a heart attack!"

A few more laughs.

That's all I'm going to be able to milk out of this one. I look down at my notes and move on.

"I saw a sign in my hotel room that said, 'A towel on the floor means I want a new one—a towel hanging up means I'll use it again.' So I called down to the front desk and asked them, 'What does a washcloth on my night table with a little bit of lotion next to it mean? I'm just asking, you seem to know what all the towel placement means . . . What? It means I'm lonely? Okay, thank you.'"

Thirty-five minutes later, the set comes to an end. The second I leave the stage, so does the adrenaline. All of my energy just evaporates and I can't seem to catch my breath. I feel like I have a massive hangover. I think I have to throw up. I step outside for air.

I still can't catch my breath, so I stumble back inside, put my hands on my knees, and stare at the carpet. It is absolutely the filthiest carpet I've ever seen. I spend a couple of seconds thinking about how many other performers have stood on this rug, spilling beer and ashing cigarettes into the crusty fibers.

The carpet suddenly looks like the most comfortable resting place in the world, so I sink down into it, face-first.

Sarah kneels next to me. I can tell by the way she's looking at me that she thinks I'm just stoned. The truth is I smoked about a half a joint before I went onstage. It's not something I usually do—a couple of years ago I did the same thing before a show in Seattle and had a panic attack. Now that I think about it, the symptoms were almost exactly the same.

Sarah was there that night and remembers as well as I do. "Is Todd feeling nauseous?" she asks.

I let out something that's halfway between a grunt and a moan.

"Poor baby," she continues. "Do you want some scrambled warm eggs? I can make them extra runny!" I bang the rug a couple of times with my hand. "Is that your way of telling me you think that was funny?"

It was. I'm glad that she understands because I seem to have lost the ability to speak.

Now Jeff Ross is standing next to her. "Let me take your shoes off for you," he says. He slips the shoes off my feet and then pinches his nose in fake disgust. "Let me put your shoes back on for you."

This time I let out a muted cackle. "Aww, look," Sarah says. "He gave you a mercy laugh."

"No it wasn't!" I manage to croak.

At this point I hear Jon Hamm screaming at the top of his lungs:

"Will someone call a goddamn ambulance? Or are we all just going to sit here and watch Todd die?"

Okay, Jon Hamm wasn't there, but give me a break: I'm just

trying to move some books. And by the way, if the imaginary Jon Hamm in my story cared so much, why didn't *he* call the ambulance? Like he doesn't have a cell phone? Typical Hamm—I love the guy to death, but he's always bossing people around. Anyway, he wasn't there, so let's move on.

There's something clearly wrong with me. But I know that it's not a heart attack. I'd be puking all over myself. Or unconscious. Trust me, I've spent a lot of time thinking about heart attacks. Heart troubles run on both sides of my family. My dad was forty-five when he died. Which is kind of funny when you think about it: I just turned forty-five a couple of months ago.

"Todd, I think we should call an ambulance," Sarah says.

I'm probably just having another panic attack. In a few minutes I'm going to feel like an idiot for scaring the crap out of everybody. "No ambulance!" I say, worrying less about my health than my insurance plan's $5,000 deductible.

Sarah leans down and whispers in my ear: "Oh, honey, don't worry, we'll pay for it! But it will have to be your birthday *and* Christmas present, is that okay?"

I give her the best laugh I can, which at this point isn't much. I hear Jeff Ross telling Flanagan, the owner of the club, that an ambulance is on the way. Jeff is going to look pretty fucking silly when this thing passes and I'm back onto my feet.

Minutes later, an EMT is kneeling down next to me. "Why don't we get you into the ambulance and check your vitals, maybe save a trip to the emergency room," he says. I'm not exactly in any position to argue. A small crowd has gathered around the exit, watching as I get wheeled out on a stretcher.

This is really starting to get embarrassing. A few minutes ago, I was performing for these people, feeling like I was in charge of the room. Now I feel helpless and weak. I can't wait for the medics to finish up and send me on my way. Tomorrow the whole thing is going to seem hilarious. Maybe even later tonight . . .

"Sir, I don't want to alarm you," the EMT says, "but you're having a heart attack."

Okay, maybe not tonight. *I don't want to alarm you?* If he didn't want to alarm me he should have told me I was fine. Telling someone they're having a heart attack is very goddamn alarming. "We're going to take you to Cedars," he continues. "Is there anyone we should call?"

Right. If I'm dying—which is suddenly starting to feel like a real possibility—I should probably tell the person I've been sharing a life with for the last fourteen years. I look through the faces around me until I find Sarah's. "Call *Andrea* for me," I say, trying to wink. At this point it looks more like an involuntary facial tic.

Sarah winks back. "Don't worry, I'll call . . . *Andrea*."

We both know that "Andrea" is actually Chris, my boyfriend. But there's no way in hell I'm going to say his name in front of everyone.

I mean, that might make people think that I was gay or something.

Here I am, forty-five years old, possibly at death's door, surrounded by friends—and I still can't be honest about who I am.

How the fuck did I get here?

HOW THE FUCK I GOT HERE.

CHAPTER 1
LIFE IS JUST A BOWL OF ICING

Where Todd promises himself he'll grow up into a silly adult.

It's funny how many of the memories that stick with you—the ones that shape you and make you who you are as an adult—are things that you never thought were important at the time.

Once in a while, when I was little, my mom would fix up a bowl of icing. She placed it on the kitchen table with five spoons: one for her, each of my three brothers, and for me. Obviously, we loved this little family tradition, but we didn't understand why we were so lucky.

"When I was a little girl," Mom explained, "I used to love to lick the icing off the beaters. But wouldn't a whole bowl of icing be better? And I thought, when I grow up, I'm going to give my kids bowls of icing."

Children make promises all the time about the things they're going to do when they grow up, but how many of them really follow through as adults? My mom did. Even if it was just a bowl of icing.

It was 1970. We lived in a row house on Kilburn Road in Northeast Philadelphia. My parents were social people who loved to have friends over at night. Once in a while, when my brothers and I were tucked in bed upstairs, listening to everyone laughing down below, one of the adults would come upstairs to "check on us." Occasionally this involved jumping up and down on the bed or playing some silly game with us. I remember being five years old and making a promise to myself, just like my mother did: *When I get old, I'm going to act silly, too.*

By the way, we should establish two things. First, that for me, "old" meant my parents' age, which at the time was twenty-six. Way old, right? I remember an early bit I used to do with my older brother Michael, when I was maybe eight, pretending that we were talking on the phone in the future. "Hey, Michael, I'm fifty today."

"What are you going to do today, Todd, for your fiftieth birthday?"

"Well, I guess I'll just stay in the house and shit in my pants and yell at people to get off my lawn. I mean, I'm fifty, what else would I do?"

The second thing, this being the 1970s, is that it wasn't uncommon for a joint to get passed around at these gatherings. One morning I asked my parents why they'd been laughing so hard the night before. My mom tried to explain what was so funny, obviously without mentioning the fact that they were high.

"Your father asked me, 'How come they have an extra-large and an extra-small, but there isn't an extra-medium?'" I thought it was a pretty funny joke, even if I didn't understand that their laughter had been enhanced. Years later I would put the line into my act, where it would stay for a very long time.

There were a lot of things I didn't understand as a kid that make sense to me now. Like when my dad would come into the room in the morning and say, "Hey, do you want to go to work with me?" Adding, if I showed even the slightest hesitation, "Come on! I'll let you sit in the backseat of the station wagon with the window open, just how you like. And we can get French fries at that place where you eat them with a wooden fork."

Later, I found out that these incredible acts of generosity from my dad were actually meant for my mom, who needed a time-out from listening to me. Because I liked to talk.

And talk.

I talked and I talked and I talked.

When I say I talked a lot, I mean I never shut the fuck up. My parents, to their credit, never told me to shut the fuck up. "Why don't you take a commercial break?" they would ask, in what even today feels like the gentlest and most creative way to tell me to shut up without ever once hurting my feelings.

My childhood had more commercial breaks than the Super Bowl, but they never kept my mom's mischievous streak from shining through. Sometimes when I got home from school, she would jump out of the coat closet as I opened the door, scaring the shit out of me. Years later, I asked her how she knew when I was going to walk into the house. "It wasn't easy," she said. "At first I would run into the closet when I saw your school bus coming up the street. But when you got off, you'd stop and talk to every adult you passed on the way home."

She was right. The second I got off the bus, I was like a politician doing a meet and greet. I'd stop and make conversation with every neighbor who crossed my path.

"Did you guys paint the garage? Who painted it? Why'd you choose that color? How many cars are in the garage? Are they new? Which one is new? What do you mean, 'pre-owned'? How is that different from used? So if it's used, why not just say 'used'?"

Looking back at it now, I can't help but feel bad for my mom, sitting there in the dark, waiting for me to get home. Talk about committing to a bit!

CHAPTER 2
SCHOOLED

Todd's educational journey gets off to a rough start.

I really, really didn't want to go to school. On my first day of kindergarten, as my mom was about to walk me into class, I realized that I had only one option: to run like hell.

So I did—off the school lot, across the street, into the "woods," a scraggly patch of trees that had by some miracle resisted urbanization. My mom tried to put a good face on it, giggling and laughing as she chased me down and dragged me into the classroom. I, on the other hand, spent the rest of the year moping, sitting on a toy truck that I refused to drive in any direction except reverse.

I already knew that I wasn't any good at retaining information. No matter how patiently the pilot who lived across the street from us pointed out on a map the countries that he'd flown to, I couldn't remember the names of any of them. Concentrating on schoolwork seemed impossible. I probably spent thirty minutes every day carefully breaking my pencil just so I could get up to sharpen it. Sometimes I wouldn't bother breaking it; I'd just grind a full pencil down to a nub. Which meant that I needed a new pencil, which would also need sharpening. Every second I was sharpening my pencil was another second I didn't have to sit in my chair and be bored out of my goddamn mind.

I'm being serious here. One week into school and I was already lost. I used to stare out the window—just like every other kid, I figured. *Who wouldn't rather stare out the window?* What was I staring at? Anything that didn't have to do with what was going on in the classroom. There's a bulldozer plowing dirt! Look at that janitor scraping gum off a bench! They all looked like things I'd rather be doing.

I tried faking it. By first grade, I had developed a "thoughtful" look, scrunching up my face so it looked like I was really thinking deeply about whatever was being explained to me. Unfortunately, the more interested I looked, the more details my teacher, Mrs. Merriweather, would throw at me. "Thoughtful" eventually evolved into "fake understanding"—my face lit up in a way that screamed "I get it now!" Mrs. Merriweather could quit teaching, content that she'd done her job, and I could go back to staring out the window and imagining how much better life would be if I were driving that bulldozer.

The only part of school that I enjoyed was making grown-ups laugh. By the end of first grade, I had it down to a science: Give me thirty seconds, and I could crack my teacher up. It turned out to be a surprisingly valuable skill.

Mrs. Merriweather tried so hard to help me get through the school year that I almost felt bad for her. Every week she'd move me a little closer to the front of the classroom, hoping that it would help me to concentrate. By the end of the year, when my desk was literally two inches from hers, she would actually lean over and do all my work for me.

Is it possible to fail first grade? I'm pretty sure I would have if my parents hadn't decided to move to Sunshine Road.

CHAPTER 3
THE RESOURCE ROOM

Todd learns that he's different from all the other kids.
(No, not like that!)

Unlike our old house, which had more or less been in the city, our new home in Southhampton, Pennsylvania, was on a half-acre lot in the suburbs. We actually got to see them build it. Every weekend we climbed into my parents' station wagon and drove up to watch the construction.

The street was called Sunshine Road. There was plenty of sunshine, because the developers had plowed down almost every tree in the neighborhood to make room for the houses. Still, we'd been so starved for nature that even the smallest hint of life was enough to get us worked up. On our first day in the new house, my mom woke all of us up at dawn to show us a squirrel in the yard. My older brother Michael—who was maybe eight—ran back into the house to shake me out of bed.

"Todd! Mom's not lying . . . There is a fucking squirrel in the yard!"

There was also a girl in our neighborhood who would sometimes walk past our house. Back then, most people used the word "retarded" to describe her. But we'd scream a different word when we saw her ambling up the street:

"MONSTER!"

Of course I was a kid and I didn't know any better, but I still feel guilty and embarrassed when I think about it today—even as an adult, I hope she didn't understand what we were yelling at her. It's not a memory I'm proud of. It also turned out to be more than a little bit ironic, given what was about to happen next.

The new home meant a new school and a chance for a fresh start. But as I started second grade at Davis Elementary, it didn't take long for me to figure out that my retention skills weren't getting any better.

In case you haven't already figured it out, I was—and still am—dyslexic. And to make matters worse, I also have severe attention deficit disorder.

But I didn't know any of this back then—all I knew was that my attention span was shot to shit. It still is, by the way. I can't sit still for more than a few minutes without sweating until I'm drenched or falling asleep. Forget about reading newspapers or following complicated movie plots. If I meet someone new and he starts telling me about his job, I'll be checked out before he gets halfway through.

"Come on, let me give it a shot," the guy will continue, fully confident in his ability to explain mortgage annuities in a way that would make sense to a four-year-old. "So you know that banks make loans, called mortgages?"

"Yeah . . ."

"Now imagine you can take all those loans and combine them into . . ."

Cue my thoughtful face. *Now hold it . . . Hold it . . . Hold it . . . That should do the trick.* Close with the "I got it" face and walk away before he asks me another question.

What can I say? It's worked since kindergarten.

Some people have also told me that I have obsessive-compulsive disorder, but I think that's just because I like things to be neat and clean. If I seem a little OCD, it's probably related to the ADD and the dyslexia—I don't function very well in chaotic environments, so I do my best to get rid of chaos whenever I can. People sometimes are quick to label you OCD if you're an organized person. I don't think that's fair. I know a lot of people who are messy and I don't immediately assume they're pigs. "You don't like to do your dishes right after you eat? You must be a filthy pig!"

Look, I know a lot of people think that kids today are over-diagnosed. Undoubtedly some of them are. But there are plenty of kids who are legitimately suffering and need help. Even now, dyslexia is not an easy condition to diagnose.

When I failed—and seriously, folks, who fails second grade unless they're suffering from some kind of serious issue?—I began third grade in the Resource Room.

The Resource Room was a catchall for the students who couldn't keep pace with the rest of the class. Today we try to act a little more enlightened in the way we treat our kids. We don't lump dyslexics together with the kids who are suffering from Down syndrome or autism—each of these conditions has its own form of treatment. But in the 1970s, we were all grouped together.

What the kids in the Resource Room did have in common is that none of us responded well to classroom teaching, so we spent a lot of time outside of the classroom. We were always walking somewhere on some kind of class trip, where we could at least get some kind of visual stimulation to keep us from tearing the room to pieces. When we passed the open doors of the other classrooms—past the kids who had been my classmates a year earlier—I tried to slip into the middle of the pack to make myself invisible. Unfortunately, I wasn't the only one with that plan—almost every other kid in my class wanted to hide in the middle, too. So we pushed, we pulled, and we shoved, moving through the halls like the least coordinated marching band in the world. Needless to say, my efforts to avoid drawing attention didn't really work out the way I had hoped.

And kids being kids, well, now I was the one who was getting called names.

To be honest, the names didn't bother me all that much. While I didn't know at the time that I was dyslexic, I was pretty sure that I wasn't retarded. I might have trouble with reading and math or focusing on anything for more than twenty seconds, but I knew that I wasn't as bad off as the girl who walked through our neighborhood, or even some of the other kids in the Resource Room. So the mean kids never really got to me.

No, what made me break into a sweaty panic attack were the *nice* kids. The ones who weren't in any way trying to be cruel, but were just curious about the mysterious, uncoordinated mob who seemed to be living totally outside of the normal school experience.

"Why are you in that room?" they'd always ask nicely. "What are you?"

I didn't know. Neither did my teachers. Their overall strategy was pretty much the same for every kid in the Resource Room: They tried to figure out what underlying emotional problems kept us from keeping up with the rest of the class.

Sometimes they'd bring in outside therapists. I remember one who had us draw pictures of life at home. Here was this guy who had never met me before, asking in his most pleasantly condescending tone of voice if the boy I'd drawn was happy.

"No."

"No?"

"No. His parents beat him."

The therapist paused thoughtfully. "Todd, do your parents beat you?"

"Of course not! You asked me about the kid in the picture. His parents are nuts."

Like always I tried to keep my teachers amused. During one of our class trips, I asked Mrs. Biazzi if she wanted to hear a joke.

"I had a dream last night that I was in a room and there were all these clocks . . ." This was a joke I'd heard from my oldest brother, Spencer. I knew from watching him that I should try to keep my delivery natural. "There was this guy there and I asked him what all these clocks were for. He told me that every time a clock's hands go all the way around, somebody has just jerked off."

Mrs. Biazzi's jaw dropped to the floor, which I took to be a good sign. Time to deliver the punch line—I wanted to tie it to someone we knew, so I chose my classmate Dennis. "So I asked the guy in the dream where Dennis's clock was, and he told me they kept it in the attic where they used it as a fan."

I still can't believe Mrs. Biazzi let me finish the joke, although, looking back now, I realize that she was just out of college. What twenty-three-year-old isn't going to let an eight-year-old finish a joke about jerking off?

I don't know whether my teachers thought I was "cured" or were just sick of my shtick, but in fourth grade I found myself back in a regular classroom. Once again, my teachers tried desperately to help me, doing everything they could to get me through the year. They used to give out awards to encourage kids to do well in school. It makes me laugh to this day when I think about them, huddling together in the teachers' lounge, trying to figure out which award to present to me. Least Attentive? Excellence in Window-Gazing? Most Pencils Sharpened?

My parents had the same problem—whenever they used to brag about their kids they would always struggle to find a way to say something nice about me. "Let's see . . . Michael got straight A's, Spencer is joining a fraternity this year, and Corey's baseball team just won the championship. And look at Todd . . . What an appetite! He ate a whole pizza all by himself!"

When I failed fourth grade, my teachers weren't entirely sure what to do with me, but my parents saved them the trouble of having to figure it out by moving again.

CHAPTER 4
LUMPY MASHED POTATOES

Todd learns a few valuable lessons.

A few years ago my brother Spencer and I drove through Churchville, the neighborhood we moved to when I was eleven. I pointed to a modest mound of dirt that was almost hidden among the houses.

"Wow . . . I guess they mowed down the old hill."

Spencer squinted at me. "What do you mean?"

"That mound of dirt. That used to be the hill, that giant hill we used to play on."

"The hill hasn't changed, Todd."

"No no no no no . . . They must have . . ."

Of course Spencer was right. The hill hadn't changed, I had. My eleven-year-old perception of the world had developed a lot since then. As it turned out, there were plenty of things that I thought were true back then that turned out to be misconceptions. Like, for example . . .

EVERYBODY'S ON TO ME.

The house was in a new development called Woodgate. Unlike our previous neighborhood, where anything green had been clear-cut to make room for the houses, whoever built Woodgate tried to keep the natural environment intact. We had trees and leaves and a creek that ran next to our house. Compared to Sunshine Road, it felt like we were living in the forest.

I started fifth grade at Fred J. Stackpole Elementary, where all I wanted to do was to fit in. I wanted to be in a regular class. I wanted to make regular friends. I promised myself that I'd focus harder this time and really try to pass.

"Hey," one of my new classmates greeted me. "Didn't you used to go to Davis Elementary?"

"Yeah," I cautiously admitted. "In third grade."

"So did my friend James Kirkland. Did you know him?"

I immediately started to panic. I didn't know his friend, because his friend probably attended regular classes. Now this kid was going to know that I spent the year in the Resource Room. Any chance I had for a fresh start was going to be gone before it even had a chance to begin. I shook my head "no" and quickly shifted the conversation to something else.

If you smoke cigarettes, it's kind of funny to look back on your first puff—how you didn't realize it at the time, but you were beginning a habit that would go on for years. This little white lie was a similar moment in my life—the moment when I realized I could shift conversations away from topics I was trying to hide.

And so a new habit was born. Over the years I've become completely ruthless in the ways I use it. I won't think twice about faking an injury or spilling a drink on an innocent bystander if it will help me get out of a question that I'm too uncomfortable to answer. I'd pour hot coffee on your baby if you asked me when I was going to meet a nice girl and settle down.

As it turned out, I was just being paranoid. This kid wasn't trying to poke holes in my story. My fresh start remained intact. I gutted out the school year, faking everyone into believing that I was learning. And my plan probably would have worked, except . . .

I FAILED FIFTH GRADE BECAUSE OF LUMPY MASHED POTATOES.

My parents knew I needed help. After school, I'd sometimes visit with a friend of my mom's, a teacher, who worked with me on my homework. She was great—nice, smart, and surprisingly helpful with my studies. Sometimes she even cooked dinner for me after we were done.

"How do you like it?" she asked me as I chowed down.

"Good," I replied. "Except for the mashed potatoes. They're a little lumpy."

"Lumpy?"

I wasn't trying to be a dick. I thought I was being honest. I liked my potatoes fluffy, the way my mom made them, and I told her so.

"You take that back!" she said.

"What?!"

"Take it back, or you're not getting any dessert."

I refused. There was no way I was going to sacrifice my integrity at the altar of lumpy mashed potatoes just to get ahead in life. That was the last time she ever made dinner for me—or helped me with my studies—and I failed fifth grade, all because I couldn't keep my fucking mouth shut about her lumpy mashed potatoes.

But what kind of monster ruins a kid's life over mashed potatoes? I may not have been able to retain any of what I was learning at school, but I had learned an even more valuable lesson:

ADULTS AREN'T ALWAYS THE SMARTER ONES.

My obsession with landscaping began in third grade. There was something about the job that fascinated me. I'd sit for hours, pretending to smoke a pretzel stick like a cigarette, watching our local landscaper—give him fifteen minutes and a truckful of sod, and he could transform a bare patch of dirt into a thriving lawn. He was almost like a god, taking chaos and turning it into something beautiful.

But I couldn't stand the way he just carelessly threw his tools into the back of his pickup truck. Maybe I was only eight, but I knew that professionals were supposed to store their tools on frames built out of two-by-fours. And that his truck should have the name of his company painted on it. It burned me up, until one day I couldn't take it anymore. I stubbed out my pretzel stick, marched over, and told him everything that he was doing wrong.

About a week later, I saw him again. "Hey, Todd!" he called out to me. "I took your suggestions."

The frame looked half-assed, dangerous, and unstable. He'd done the lettering on his truck with a stencil—even to a kid with a reading disability, it was clear he'd done a shitty, unprofessional job. But there he was, beaming with pride, clearly looking for my approval. "What do you think?"

It turns out I'd learned something from the mashed potato incident with the tutor. "Looks great," I lied.

CHAPTER 5
JEWS IN CHURCHVILLE

Todd learns that some adults really are delusional.

Some of our new neighbors in Churchville were kind enough to welcome us to the area by throwing pennies at Michael and Spencer. "Go fetch it, Jew!" one of them yelled. A few days later, someone slashed the tires on our station wagon.

"It's a shame," one of our neighbors said, an elderly man who shook his head sadly. "I know Jews. Jews are good people."

Even then, I can remember thinking that while I appreciated what he was trying to say, he was wrong. *Jews are not all good people. They're like everybody else: Some are good, some are bad.*

It turned out the anti-Semitism was just getting started. One day we came home to find slurs written on our windows. The whole experience felt particularly weird to me because we

weren't exactly the most Jewish family in the world. We cel-
ebrated Christmas, stringing lights around the house and decorating a tree that we placed in the window. If you were going to
hate us for being Jewish, you had to really hate Jews. I mean, the
only way we could have been less Jewish was to actually not be
Jewish, which as far as I could tell was out of our hands.

I don't mean to say that everyone in Churchville hated
Jews. I'm sure that the majority of the people in the neighborhood were not anti-Semitic. But the majority of the people
didn't come to our defense. Some of them probably didn't know
what was going on.

But I'm sure some of them did.

That's why today if I see someone being mistreated I try to
find opportunities to speak up. It doesn't have to be a major civil
rights violation. If I happen to witness someone being rude or
offensive to a waitress or a cashier, I say something. I think it's
important to get involved, even in situations that don't involve
you personally. Sometimes all it takes is another person saying,
"Hey, you can't talk to her that way. She's doing her best . . ." to
snap someone out of it or to make someone else's day by coming to his or her defense.

But none of our new neighbors spoke up as the harassment
continued to escalate. My older brothers got the worst of it. They
were teased all the time at school. It got so bad that—when the
school administration failed to do anything about it—my parents filed a lawsuit against the district.

My parents also brought in the big guns: the Jewish Defense League. These guys did not fuck around. "You show us
a hand that threw a penny at you," they promised, "and we'll
break it."

Fortunately it never came to that. My parents never went through with the lawsuit—it seemed like too much of an ordeal to put my brothers and me through. As sixth grade came to a close, we did what Jews have been doing for centuries: We moved, hoping to find a more accepting neighborhood.

CHAPTER 6
OCD
IN
BLOOM

Todd finds his dream house.

If there was one thing I could always count on as a kid, it was having a house that was tidy and organized. My mom was a compulsive cleaner. Everything had its place. Dust never had a chance to settle in our home.

But when we moved into our new house in Lafayette Hill, I started to notice that my mom had developed a new tolerance for disorder. Now, as an adult, I can see that she was probably just letting go of a lot of unhealthy compulsion, embracing my aunt Ruth's philosophy that while your dishes won't leave, your company will.

But as a kid, I felt like my world was falling apart around me. I had enough trouble concentrating when things were orderly. I hated the fingerprints all over the cabinets. I missed the reassuring vacuum marks on the carpet. A dirty glass in the sink could ruin my afternoon. Things got even worse once I started sharing a room with my brother Corey.

Let me make this clear to you (and to Corey, who's probably reading this right now): By any reasonable standard, my younger brother was a normal ten-year-old boy, no messier than most kids his age. I could list the things he did that drove me nuts, but that would only highlight how crazy I was. I looked at Corey and I saw a hoarder—I'm not talking about the high-class HGTV kind, but an A&E, living-in-your-own-filth-with-three-dead-cats-under-your-bed type.

My issues didn't go away when the room was clean. I'd find any excuse to vacuum, making one up if I had to. "Ugh," I'd say, after intentionally dropping a plant on the rug, allowing some of the dirt to spill. "Which one of the dogs did this? I guess I better get the vacuum cleaner."

When Corey's hair started falling out, I knew it wasn't (as my parents told me) because of an allergy, but from the stress of having to live with me. He moved across the hall to bunk with Spencer, and I got my own room, where I could enforce my insane standards of clean.

To my family's great credit, they all did their best to appease my craziness. But I was about to meet people who really understood me—our neighbors across the street, the Nalibotskys.

Like we had with our previous home in Churchville, we made a few visits to Lafayette Hill to see our new home being built. On one of these trips I noticed the mini-mansion that was going up across the street. *Holy shit—they've got a three-car garage! And a circular driveway! They must be rich!*

To this day, the things I saw the Nalibotskys do represent to me what "rich people" do. Rich people roll their towels. Rich people don't leave their mops to air-dry outside the kitchen door. Rich people don't keep their dish soap on their kitchen sink. As funny as it might seem, I'm not wrong about this—when was the last time you opened *Architectural Digest* and saw a $5 million home with Palmolive on the sink next to an old sponge full of bacon grease? Yeah, that's what I thought. (By the way, if the people at Palmolive want to send me a case for free, I'll drop this bit out of the act.)

I know now that you can also have all the money in the world and still not get it. Lots of rich people have terrible taste. Either way, the Nalibotskys got it.

Keep in mind, the Glass family wasn't exactly doing without. My dad owned a successful wholesale shoe business. We were comfortable, building a very nice house in the suburbs for the fourth time in the last five years. But I became obsessed with the house across the street.

The landscaping was immaculate, like something you'd see in a magazine. The lawn was a perfect shade of green, the driveway freshly sealed and free of cracks. Everything was arranged in clean lines and rows, separated by crisp edges and railroad ties. In time, I found out that it belonged to Phil Nalibotsky, the builder behind the new development. He held on to three or four of the lots to build what was probably his dream home. Little did he know he was building twelve-year-old Todd Glass's dream home, too.

I still fantasize about it today. If I ever decide to buy a summer home, I'm going to be the only person in the world who owns a vacation property in Lafayette Hill, Pennsylvania. You'll know it when you see my dream car in the driveway: a '77 Ford LTD with wood paneling and lights that open and close.

I had to see the inside of that house. Maybe if I crashed my bike in their driveway they'd nurse me back to health. I could track down their lost dog (after letting it out myself) or save them from a fire (that I may or may not have started). Eventually I dismissed all of these ideas (especially the last—how was I going to see the inside of their house if it was on fire?) and went for a more direct approach: I walked up and knocked on their front door.

I was glad that I did. I didn't know anything about design or decorating, but there was something about the inside of the house that immediately made me feel calm. The sense of order was incredible: zero clutter; everything had its place. You'd never know that three kids were living there. Unlike the other houses in the neighborhood, which all seemed to be carpeted with randomly colored wall-to-wall shag, the Nalibotskys' home used themes that made each room feel like it was connected to the rest. Years later, Mrs. Nalibotsky—Myra—explained to me that she'd hired a decorator who believed that there was "beauty in unity and simplicity."

When Phil got home from work, he walked right to the kitchen sink to put away whatever few dishes were sitting there. Keep in mind—this is a family that had full-time help in the housekeeping department. "I noticed that the hose was un-raveled outside," he said to his kids. "Did someone forget to roll it back up?"

His kids were obviously annoyed by the observation. All I could think was: *This guy gets it.* I still think that way today, organizing my house as if Phil and Myra might stop by at any time. There aren't any sponges full of bacon grease. I don't leave dishes in the sink. I keep a laminated list of frequently used numbers hanging in my kitchen, just like the Nalibotskys did, a totally unnecessary gesture given that I've got them all stored on my cell.

Shortly after my bar mitzvah, my parents left us alone for a weekend, figuring we were in good hands with our neighbor's daughter babysitting us. I remember standing in the middle of the street watching the landscapers tend to the Nalibotskys' perfect yard. Then I turned to face our house and its perfectly ordinary grass lawn. Back to theirs, back to ours. Back to theirs . . .

This went on for an hour until, finally, I knew what I had to do. I strode over to the landscaper in charge. "I want our yard to look like theirs," I said.

It's funny to look back now and try to imagine what was going through this guy's mind. *He obviously doesn't own the home . . . unless he's the most successful thirteen-year-old I've ever met.* I told him that my parents had left me in charge of the house. More importantly, I showed him cash—almost a thousand dollars from my bar mitzvah. I guess if a thirteen-year-old hired me to do stand-up comedy and paid cash, I wouldn't ask any questions, either. (Seriously, I'm not kidding—call my agent. Special discounts for Monday- and Tuesday-night bookings that won't cut into my comedy club schedule.)

My parents must have thought they'd come home to the wrong house. They stared at the yard, trying to process what had happened in the short time they were gone. There were new railroad ties lining the driveway. Crisp, clean-cut lines separated the grass lawn from the large piles of dark mulch that had been spread around the shrubs.

"Todd's a big man in a little man's body," the landscaper explained to my confused mom and dad. But it looked right, and my parents had to admit that I'd improved things while they were gone. My dad even said they'd repay my investment, but I don't think they ever did. So, Mom, if you're reading this . . . I'm pretty sure you owe me some money.

CHAPTER 7
THE STOMACHACHE

Fake vomit and false stereotypes.

The move to Lafayette Hill also meant I had to start all over again at another new school.

I hated it. I hated it from day one. A new group of teachers that I had to fool into thinking that I was actually learning something. A new group of kids that I had to try and make friends with, kids that I really didn't even like all that much. I felt like I had a stomachache that wouldn't go away. Unfortunately, I wasn't quite sick enough to stay home from school, not as far as my parents were concerned.

Keep in mind that when a sixth-grader—or in my case, a seventh-grader in sixth grade—fakes throwing up, he doesn't necessarily think things all the way through. I grabbed some saltines from the kitchen and crumbled them into the toilet.

The result wasn't really that convincing, so I added a few squirts of ketchup to give it a pukier feel and ran off to tell my parents.

By the time they got to the bathroom, the saltines had pretty much dissolved, leaving nothing but a thick red mess floating in the water. A few minutes later I was being rushed into the emergency room, my parents trying to stay calm while they explained to the doctors why they thought their son was bleeding internally.

At this point I was way too scared to tell anyone about the ketchup. The doctors ran tests on me. My dad skipped work so that he and my mom could sit in the waiting room.

Obviously they didn't find any internal bleeding. The only thing the doctors did find was a packet of saltines in my pocket. Did I tell my parents the truth? Of course I did . . . Just not right away. I waited until about two years ago, when I was forty-five, to confess the truth to my mom, figuring enough time had passed for us both to laugh about it. Man, was I wrong—while I'd like to say I was making this up for comedic purposes, my mother was still really upset with me. If she could have taken TV away for a week, I'm pretty sure she would have.

Once the real stomachache and fake vomiting had subsided, I was surprised to find out that I really liked sixth grade. They placed me in a program called "Open Space," which encouraged group activities and lots of social time. I seemed to be making progress. I felt like I was flourishing and, possibly, even learning a thing or two.

That didn't stop me from failing.

The next year I went to a private school called Wordsworth Academy that was known for having a great "special education" program. My parents couldn't really afford private school—the whole experience was paid for by an anonymous donor. (My guess was that my mysterious benefactors were the Nalibotskys, but if I was right, they never gave me a clue.)

Despite the generosity that got me there, my experience at Wordsworth wasn't ideal. They put me on Ritalin, which only killed my appetite, not my confusion. My new pool of potential friends was limited to kids who either had serious learning disabilities or were suffering from emotional problems that seemed a lot more severe than mine. (Although, in retrospect, it was probably perfect preparation for a lifetime of friendships with writers and stand-up comedians.)

I was old enough at this point to be absolutely terrified by my lack of progress. *Focus . . . Just FOCUS*, I'd yell at myself every time I felt my mind drifting off in the middle of class. Not an effective approach—it's almost impossible to learn algebra when all you're focusing on is focusing.

The teachers were all very nice. They tried desperately to find ways to connect with me and engage me in schoolwork. Most of them could tell I wasn't lacking intelligence, which made my academic troubles that much more frustrating for them.

One day, when I was acting particularly miserable, a teacher pointed to a sickly-looking plant on the windowsill. "Todd, what do you think is wrong with this plant?"

Now my mom had obviously told the teacher that I liked plants. This poor woman was just trying to find a way to connect with me. It's easy to see, in hindsight, that these were loving people who didn't know what to do. But the thirteen-year-old me was tired of being patronized. And besides, I didn't even like plants—I liked landscaping. Not the same thing! I wanted to say. Not even fucking close.

"It's sick," I said. "You should throw it away."

"Are you sure?" my teacher replied. "What if we gave it some water?"

"No, that plant is sick. You better throw it away before it spreads whatever it has to the rest of the plants. It'll kill them all."

"Maybe it just needs a little sun."

"What it needs is to be put out of its misery."

Outside of school, I desperately wanted to be friends with Albert Nalibotsky, who I saw as my in to becoming a part of their family. Albert and I didn't have much in common. He loved sports and would beg me all the time to go outside and toss a football. I hated sports. Whenever sports were on TV in our house, I wasn't allowed to talk, so you could forget about me being interested. Sports still represent two of my least favorite things in life: exercise and not talking.

Now stop.

I know what you're thinking.

Obsessive about cleaning? Check!

An eye for landscaping and design? Check!

Doesn't like sports? Check!

It all adds up. It was obvious, even then, that I was . . .

Bullshit!

A lot of people seem to think that being gay automatically means you're great at design, fashion, or throwing great dinner parties. This idea really bothers the hell out of me. Gay people aren't born with these particular interests or skills in their DNA; they have to learn them slowly over time, like any other interest or skill. It would be like if you met an Asian doctor and said, "No wonder you're a doctor, you're Asian! You people are smart!" Oh yeah? What about the years of medical school and thousands of hours of work and study? Did you ever take that into account, you lazy piece of shit?

You'll sometimes hear that stereotypes exist for a reason: because they're true. I don't think that's right, either. I know a lot of straight guys who, if they pretended to come out of the closet, would have people falling all over themselves to tell you how they knew it all along. "No wonder he's a great dresser and has such a beautiful home! Now it all makes sense . . ."

The truth is that some guys are good at this kind of stuff; some are not. Gay or straight doesn't have anything to do with it. Most of our "stereotypes" are simple observations that don't have any connection to what's in your DNA.

Gay guys have style? They also have two incomes and no kids.

Asians love cameras? They're on vacation in our country, fuckface!

Jews are cheap? You're right, everyone else loves to overpay for shit.

So an eye for design and a dislike for sports didn't mean that I was gay. However, there was one small detail that might have hinted that something about me was a little bit different: I started to have feelings for guys.

Which, I've got to admit, sounds pretty gay.

CHAPTER 8

GAY LIKE ME

Just when it couldn't get any worse . . .

Look, discovering sexuality is hard enough for kids to go through when it's accepted by everybody. If a boy likes a girl, and he's thirteen and she's thirteen, dipping their toes (and whatever else) into a heterosexual relationship embraced by society, it's already so difficult. Holy shit are there feelings to go through. Feelings that are complicated and new and weird and exciting and terrifying.

Now imagine going through this process and also feeling dirty about it.

But I'm getting ahead of myself.

By the time I was thirteen, I *knew*. Sometimes I would see a guy and I'd feel a sense of attraction for him. I also knew enough not to say a word about it to anybody.

We're talking about the late 1970s. While I wasn't necessarily sure what my feelings meant, I was old enough to know that words like "gay," "fag," and "homo" were insults.

I should point out that I was a lucky kid in that none of these prejudices came from my parents, who socialized with people of every race, religion, sexual orientation, and economic class. But I grew up in the same straight world as everyone else did. If you could hide being gay, you did. And even if you couldn't, you still did. (One word: Liberace.) I learned that "normal" people got uncomfortable when they saw same-sex couples, so I did, too. Whenever other boys my age started to talk about the crushes they were developing on girls, I immediately clammed up. I was pretty sure that my own weird feelings would go away. I just had to hide them until that happened.

One night I stayed over at a friend's house. We were watching TV and our legs touched.

We didn't say very much after that. There wasn't any kissing, just a lot of groping. "Heavy petting" is the phrase that comes to mind—the kind of stuff you might expect a thirteen-year-old boy and a thirteen-year-old girl to do. It felt good. It felt right.

And when I woke up the next morning, it felt dirty.

I can't say that I handled it poorly, because I didn't handle it at all. I went out of my way not to see him again. I breathed a huge sigh of relief when, a few months later, he moved away, so I could get on with the business of forgetting that it had ever happened.

I mean, what the fuck? I was failing out of school and didn't know what was wrong with me, met people who hated me for being part of a religion that I hardly practiced, had been to five different schools in eight years leaving me with almost no close friends, and now I was going to have to be gay, too?

I must have been a real asshole in my past life to deserve all that in this one.

CHAPTER 9
THE POWER OF FUNNY

A comedian is born.

The last thing I want to do is to make my childhood sound more dramatic than it was. While I might get a little sad or angry when I look back on it, at the time, life seemed pretty good. I didn't walk around depressed every day. Kids are resilient. I laughed a lot.

I always had a lot of fun with my family, and a lot of that fun revolved around comedy. My dad used to watch *Fernwood 2Night*— a show that was crazy ahead of its time—so he clearly had an evolved sense of humor. I didn't necessarily get all the jokes, but I loved Martin Mull and Fred Willard, who could sell all sorts of funny with an upturned eyebrow or a deadpan expression.

Later, my brothers and I became obsessed with *The Carol Burnett Show*. Michael and Spencer learned all of the Eunice and

Ed Higgins sketches by heart and would spend hours cracking me up.

Comedy was something I could relate to. I didn't have to read anything. Even if I didn't understand everything that the performers were saying, I liked the way they were saying it. They used their voices, going louder or quieter, speaking faster or slower, to create a mood and tell a story—it was a way of communicating that really resonated with me.

Every day I'd come home from school and watch *Mike Douglas* or *Merv Griffin*, two talk shows that usually ended with a stand-up routine, hoping to see comedians like Rodney Dangerfield or Don Rickles. When Spencer got a George Carlin album, we played the hell out of it. Not only was Carlin hilarious, but it felt like he was talking right to us, telling the truth in a way that other adults couldn't or wouldn't.

Pretty soon, without even realizing it, I was starting to think like a comedian. I still remember the very first time I used irony to take a piece of information and turn it around in a way that highlighted how ridiculous it was. I was in the car with my parents and someone cut us off. "Sometimes I wish I had an old clunker so I could just plow into people," my dad complained to no one in particular.

"Yeah, that's a great idea, Dad. You think if you ran someone off the road and they called the cops, the cops would be like, 'Sorry . . . Nothing we can do about this one. He clearly has an old clunker. We're going to have to let him go.'"

I knew I'd done well when I heard my mom crack up from the passenger seat.

Meanwhile, since we'd been in the same house for a couple of years, it was obviously time for the Glass family to move again. This time we ended up in Valley Forge, which really felt way out in the country. The house was down a quarter-mile gravel driveway that led to a twenty-five-acre ranch—we lived on what was maybe two and a half acres on the back of the lot.

When you're living in the middle of nowhere and you're not into organized sports, it isn't that easy to make new friends. But I found one at my new school, a kid named Blake who let me copy from him when we were taking tests. He was so gracious. He never did what some people do, moving their hand to cover the page—as a matter of fact, he'd even move the paper closer to the edge of his desk to make it easier for me. The only problem, I realized pretty quickly, was that I was copying from a straight-D student.

I figured I should probably find some smarter friends. Taking a page from the comedians I'd been watching and listening to, I tried to use my sense of humor. It wasn't always successful. We were reading a book at school called *Hey, Dummy*. Later, while riding in the car with my brother, I saw one of my classmates and wanted to make him laugh, so I yelled at him: "Hey, dummy!"

When I ran into him at school the next day and saw how pissed he was, I panicked and denied that it was me. He panicked and punched me in the face. This was a great lesson in comedy: Know your crowd.

But I was starting to see how a sense of humor could improve my social life. My first impression of Joe Greco, the kid who sat behind me in my new homeroom, was that he was kind of a tough guy. One morning, my new homeroom teacher announced that they were still looking for the lead in the school musical. All of a sudden Joe chimed in, singing, "I'llllllllllll *do it!*"

His delivery was perfect, but no one else in the class even

chuckled. I, on the other hand, fell on the floor laughing. I still laugh when I think about it now.

A few days later, Joe got the chance to return the favor. My current obsession was Rodney Dangerfield. I'd recently bought his album and had spent hours mimicking his routine until I felt comfortable enough to try a few jokes out in class, replacing Rodney's wife with my mother: "My mom is such a bad cook, in my house we pray *after* we eat. Guys, seriously, it's really bad . . . The other day I caught a fly fixing the screen door!"

And . . . crickets. Except for Joe, who gave me what I thought was a pity laugh.

One of my classmates sneered at him. "You think he's funny?"

"Yeah," Joe said, in a voice that made the kid cower in the corner. "I do."

And just like that, somebody my age thought I was funny.

What was amazing was that Joe wasn't the only person who seemed to think so. The most popular kid in my class, Dave Olsen, started acting like he wanted to be my friend, too. Everybody liked Dave—he was smart, friendly, and got along with all different kinds of people.

I didn't really understand why he was being so nice to me until years later, during a visit to his house, when his dad said, "Dave, don't forget—remember to be friends with someone who doesn't have any friends!"

"Wait a minute," I said, looking at Dave. "That's *me*! You became my friend in high school because you felt sorry for me."

Dave denied it, but I was smart enough to know what was up. And at that point, who cared? We'd already become friends, which still amazes me. A lot of teenagers use their popularity for evil. But if you want your kid to be really, truly cool, teach him or her to use popularity for good, like Dave Olsen did.

I can't overstate how great it felt to have a friend like Dave. For the first time in my life, I was looking forward to going to school. I liked having friends. We had a good time doing the kinds of crazy things that high school kids did. My friend Jamie bought a used unmarked police car. It didn't take long to notice that the other cars on the road were slowing down when we pulled behind them. "Oh!" it finally dawned on us. "They think we're cops."

So we started pulling people over. No one who looked dangerous, just kids about our age who were doing something erratic—there's nothing more fun than catching someone in the middle of doing something stupid. We'd flash the high beams and the car would pull over. Jamie and I both looked a lot older than our age; later we'd wear blue windbreakers and tuck them into our pants, just like we saw cops do, before we approached the driver. "How ya doing? You know, the reason we have unmarked cars is so we can catch people doing the kinds of things that you were doing . . ."

Look, as a full-grown adult, this is an embarrassing story—we were in it for the power and the fun. After we were done scaring the crap out of some poor kid, we'd get back into Jamie's car and giggle like no real cop ever would. It was a great gag, at least until it came to a screeching halt when, one day on the way to school, we accidentally pulled over the principal.

For the first time in my life, I was really enjoying school. I was having a great time with my new friends and there was no way I was going to mess it up. Any romantic feelings I had for guys got pushed into the back of my mind where I hoped and prayed that they'd stay.

CHAPTER 10
DIM PROSPECTS

School is coming to an end.

Having friends made high school a lot more fun, but it wasn't like I was suddenly going to become a better student. When (big surprise) I failed tenth grade, I seriously considered dropping out. By then it was clear to everyone around me (and, most importantly, me) that college wasn't an option. We would have had to move to Mongolia to get away from my school record.

I probably would have quit out of sheer embarrassment if one of my teachers, Mr. Smedley, hadn't felt sorry enough for me to let me walk into assembly room with my eleventh-grade friends, allowing me to hold on to some small shred of dignity before heading off to repeat the same lessons that I still wouldn't be able to retain.

But my school days were coming to an end. What the hell was I going to do?

Fortunately, I had a dream: I wanted to be a landscaper like Comar.

Comar ran his own landscaping business, but he never seemed to have to do any of the backbreaking labor that should have come with the job. He'd pull up to a site in his $45,000 pickup truck, climbing out to survey the scene like a king stepping out of a royal carriage. His perfectly pressed shirt was always tucked neatly into his immaculately spotless pants. The few times I saw Comar pick up a hose, there were three guys standing behind him to make sure it didn't get knotted or caught on anything that might have required the boss to over-exert himself.

I wanted to be Comar. In the meantime, however, I had to settle for an after-school job at Dairy Queen in the Plymouth Meeting Mall. I loved that job. I was great at it, at least from the perspective of the customers. I made sure that people got as much ice cream as I could fit into whatever size they ordered—I'd stuff a small so full that it'd be larger than a medium. It brought me a lot of joy to bring that kind of happiness to others.

The feelings of joy didn't extend to the owners, who more than once had warned me to weigh the portions like everyone else did. But I knew I was doing important work. I wore a clean, pressed shirt to work every day, tucked neatly into my pants, and occasionally lied to customers about being the owner's son. Unlike the other sixteen-year-old slobs working for minimum wage, I showed up an hour early to work to bring the place up to my personal (and arguably insane) standards. I stopped serving milkshakes—man, what a mess—a half hour before closing; fifteen minutes later I'd put all the chairs up on the tables to encourage the last customers of the day to take their orders to go.

I wasn't sure that the owners would fully appreciate the extra effort it took to close early, so I doled out free ice cream to the mall's security guards to buy their silence. Their loyalty was put to the test when, twenty minutes before closing time, I refused to serve a milkshake to Angie, a forty-year-old who still worked at the Piercing Pagoda kiosk, and she ratted me out to my bosses.

The security guards came through for me, denying any knowledge of early closures, and the owners were happy to let it go. Not so much me—I didn't want to do any damage that would be permanent, but I definitely had to teach Angie a lesson in the dynamics of power. I should explain that the Piercing Pagoda, being a kiosk, didn't have its own bathroom, and I occasionally saved Angie the humiliation of using the public restrooms by letting her use our private toilet at the Dairy Queen. But that was before she decided to double-cross me. The next time she ordered a milkshake, I added three doses of Ex-Lax.

Let me tell you, when you're sixteen, there aren't many things in life as pleasurable as watching a full-grown adult who really has to take a shit. The few minutes I watched her squirm were pure enjoyment. I never found out what happened next, because I closed early and went home.

There was a bar next door to the Dairy Queen where musicians would occasionally play. For some reason—possibly because I was a sixteen-year-old who looked thirty—no one seemed to mind when I'd wander up to the stage after work, grab the mike, and break into my Rodney routine.

I was just goofing off. While I knew there were famous comedians, I didn't have any idea that "stand-up comedy" could
be an actual job until the night I got a call from my old friend
and neighbor Albert Nalibotsky, inviting me to check out a club
he'd recently discovered.

CHAPTER 11
COMEDY WORKS

"Mr. and Mrs. Schleinheffer, please call your babysitter immediately. She wants to know where you keep the fire extinguisher."

Comedy Works was on the third floor of a three-story walk-up, above a Middle Eastern restaurant on Chestnut Street. The stairs opened into a long, narrow room that held around three hundred people. A few minutes after Albert and I sat down, the room went dark. "Before we start tonight's show," a voice announced over the PA system, "if there's a Mr. and Mrs. Schleinheffer in the audience tonight, a Mr. and Mrs. Schleinheffer, please call your babysitter immediately. She wants to know where you keep the fire extinguisher. Other than that, everything's okay. Five minutes to showtime . . ."

I laughed at that goddamn announcement for a month.

But that was just the beginning. The owner of the club, a guy named Steve Young, kicked off what was for me about to become a familiar routine. He introduced the master of ceremonies—the emcee—usually a local comic just starting to work the clubs. The emcee did a few minutes of comedy before introducing the middle act, who tonight was the Legendary Wid, famous for using 250 props during his show. It was total mayhem—by the end of his act there were piles of one-off props everywhere. It was too huge a mess to clean up right away, so management threw a couple of blankets over the props so the headliner could begin—a rising twenty-year-old named Tom Wilson, who a few years later would play "Biff" in *Back to the Future*.

To say that the night left an impression on me would be an understatement. I felt so exhilarated I couldn't contain it. I went back the following Friday. This time, Gilbert Gottfried was the headliner. His act was kind of a riff on comedic conventions, making fun of the generic routines that some stand-ups do. I felt like most of the audience didn't get it, but I did. I laughed so hard I almost hyperventilated.

I wasn't just hooked—I became obsessed with Comedy Works. I'd start talking about it every Monday morning at school: "Who wants to go to the Comedy Works? Who wants to go to the Comedy Works?"

Keep in mind that this was 1981. Comedy clubs were something that happened in New York or L.A. I couldn't believe that a place like this existed in Philadelphia. For five dollars, I got to see young, relatively unknown comics like Eddie Murphy, Steven Wright, Richard Lewis, Roseanne Barr, and Tim Allen, not to mention up-and-coming stars like Jay Leno, Paul Reiser, and Jerry Seinfeld.

I wanted to be in the front row at the first show every Friday night. After school I'd grab any friends I could find and barrel eighty miles an hour down the Schuylkill Expressway to beat the traffic. If, after the first show ended, I happened to run into some more friends who were on line for the late show, I would shell out another five dollars to join them. One night, Steve Young pulled me aside—he'd noticed me moving back in line for a second show and let me in for free. I couldn't believe that the club's owner knew who I was. I was so happy that I nearly had a nervous breakdown.

At almost every show, Steve would make an announcement: "Hey, if you think you're funny, Wednesday night is our open mike night. Why not try your hand at comedy?" After about five months of weekly visits to the club, I decided I was ready. I dragged all my friends to the show . . .

. . . and chickened out.

A week later, I got up the nerve to try again. This time I made it onto the stage. "I hate how they put the car horn so close to the windshield wipers," I said. "You go to honk at someone and you end up washing your windshield. It would be scarier to throw yarn out your window."

I may have been a sixteen-year-old spraying whipped cream at my brothers in the crowd and telling jokes about *The Brady Bunch*, but on that night, I killed.

Flush with success I decided to go back for more a week later. This time I invited everyone I could—and I bombed. I've talked to plenty of other comedians who have had the same experience, acing their first time onstage and flailing the next. I don't know why it happens—maybe your first time out, you have a certain sense of vulnerability that the audience can sense. Succeed, and some of that vulnerability is gone, making the laughs harder to come by.

But if you're meant to do comedy nothing will stop you. Comedy is like sex: treacherous. You have to hang out with people you normally wouldn't, doing things that take you out of your comfort zone hoping to impress them. Getting naked with strangers? If it wasn't for our built-in desire for procreation, I bet most people wouldn't dare going after sex. But that natural drive keeps us coming back for more.

I knew right away that I had a natural drive to do comedy. Bombing my second time out wasn't going to keep me away. After the show, another comic took me aside. "You were funny," he assured me. "You've just got to calm down a bit."

A few seconds after he walked away, the Legendary Wid—the man with 250 props—patted me on the back. "You don't have to calm down," he said. "Just be who you are."

CHAPTER 12
OPENING ACT

Todd gets a weekend.

I was back on the Comedy Works stage just about every Wednesday night. High school became even blurrier—on the Thursday mornings I actually showed up, I got really good at forging my dad's signature on late slips. And by then I was already counting the hours to the next show on Friday night.

I was hanging around the club so often that Steve Young decided to put me to work. I did everything, from lights to sound to keeping the flow of traffic moving up and down the narrow staircase. Steve also let me use the PA to announce that the show was about to begin. One night I decided to try my hand at a joke, the same one that had cracked me up the first night I'd visited the club.

"If there's a Mr. and Mrs. Burke in the audience, a Mr. and

Mrs. Burke, please call your babysitter immediately. She wants to know where you keep the fire extinguisher."

Suddenly I heard a woman's scream and a commotion in the audience as a terrified couple rushed for the door. It turns out the joke plays a lot better when you use a more obscure last name.

"I think you're funny," the doorman, Tony Molino, told me one night after I finished my open-mike set. "You're going to get a weekend spot soon."

That was nice of him to say, but getting a paid weekend spot was such a big deal back then that I remember thinking I wished he knew what the fuck he was talking about.

As it turned out, he did.

One afternoon, everyone was buzzing because Jay Leno was coming to Comedy Works. I'd grown up watching Jay do stand-up on *Merv Griffin* and *The John Davidson Show*. While he was still a few years away from subbing for Johnny Carson, there was no doubt that he was a legitimate star and that his show was a big deal, even for Comedy Works—tickets were selling for fifteen dollars instead of the usual five.

He was coming to Philadelphia from a club in New Jersey and someone had to go pick him up. I nearly shat in my pants when Steve asked me to do it. I borrowed my parents' station wagon and brought along two of my friends for moral support. "Whatever you do," I hissed, "don't ask any stupid questions."

Jay was friendly, but I was still incredibly nervous to have him in my car. I wanted to talk to him—about performing, about life, about anything—but I was seventeen and I was nervous and my mind went blank. The only thing I could think of was a piece of trivia I'd heard at the club: Jay always got paid in cash. "So hey," I asked him. "What do you do with your money?"

"What, are you looking for financial advice?" Jay replied.

"No," I tried to explain. "I mean where do you keep it? I heard you only got paid in cash."

My friends in the backseat started cracking up. Jay looked puzzled, wondering why we were laughing at him. I sighed and explained that I'd made my friends promise not to ask him any stupid questions.

Jay gave me a crooked smile. "Well, I guess you lowered the bar for them. So where's Steve Young? Will he be at the club?"

I explained to Jay that Steve taught a stand-up comedy class at Temple University. Jay's face lit up. "Take me there. Right now."

I strolled across campus with Jay. Everyone seemed to be staring at us. I didn't do a very good job of hiding my smile.

We got to Steve's class, where his students were taking their final exam. These kids must have been nervous enough having to do a five-minute set in front of their classmates—I can only imagine how much terror they must have felt when Jay Leno walked into the room. But Jay was incredibly supportive. He even bought a joke right on the spot from one of the girls in the class. (Which, thirty years later, I can still remember: "I Can't Believe It's Not Butter? I tried it. I can't believe it's not car wax!" Maybe not that funny now, but back then it was very topical.)

When I got back home, after dropping Jay off at his hotel, there was a message from Steve on the answering machine. "Call me," he said in a very low voice. "I might have something that would be fun for you to do tonight."

I called him back immediately. "So how would you like to open up for Jay Leno?" Steve asked.

"Tonight?" My stomach started doing somersaults.

"All the shows . . . the whole weekend."

I hung up the phone and did my best to contain my emotions. This was a big deal, a kind of validation I'd never experienced before. I sucked in school and I never scored a touchdown. But now I was not only doing something important to me, I was succeeding at it. Someone thought I was good enough to open for Jay-fucking-Leno!

The excitement lasted two minutes. Then fear set in.

I fought through my nervousness and opened the show with my best ten minutes. The middle was Tom Wilson, visiting from L.A., where he'd moved to pursue his career. Then I returned for two more minutes to do a few more jokes and to introduce the headliner.

Jay stepped out on the stage and raised his hands to quiet the cheering audience. Watching him work those nights was like going to school for me, if school had been a place where I actually learned something. Jay was a total pro—you knew it from the moment he spoke. I had already seen plenty of comedians who began their set by trying to excite the crowd: "How's everybody doing?" But Jay simply walked out, waited for the crowd to get quiet, and moved right into his routine. "I see Nancy Reagan won the Humanitarian Award this year. Good for her, I'm glad she beat out that conniving bitch Mother Teresa."

What followed were fifteen minutes of joke after joke, barely giving the audience a chance to breathe. When he finally paused to say, "How ya doing, Philadelphia?" the crowd erupted.

"And how about that Todd Glass," he said. "He's a young kid, asked me for advice. Didn't know what to tell him. Stay out of prison?"

I looked out at the audience, spotting my parents and friends. I felt great. I'd finally found a place where I belonged.

CHAPTER 13
SPRUCE STREET

Where Todd encounters swarming gays.

The end of my senior year was approaching. I knew I wasn't going to graduate with any kind of diploma, but that didn't seem as daunting or scary anymore. The fear of not knowing what to do was gone. I couldn't wait to get started with my new life.

Comedy Works had become a regular paying gig. It was starting to feel strange living at home with my parents, so I decided to move into an apartment in Center City with some other young comedians from the club. There were only two problems with the new arrangement: Parking was a nightmare and the apartment was on Spruce Street.

Spruce Street, I quickly learned after moving in, was Philadelphia's gay street. It sounds so funny—somehow different cities end up with different streets that are notoriously gay. And somehow, as chance would have it, I ended up living there.

Everywhere I looked, guys were holding hands with guys. Girls were holding hands with girls. When I couldn't find a parking space nearby, I'd have to walk four or five blocks through this scene. *Is this who I am?* I thought to myself. *Is this who I'm going to be?*

Again, keep in mind that it was 1983. AIDS was emerging as a deadly disease, but we had a president who wouldn't even mention it by name.

If everyone had been able to be open about who they were, I would have known that gay people come in all stripes. But the few gays I saw on TV or in popular culture tended to feel like caricatures to me, all affected speech and effeminate mannerisms. The people I passed on Spruce Street seemed to behave the same way.

"I don't care that they're gay," I complained one night to my roommates. "But why do they have to be such a parody?"

"I'm sure there are all kinds of gay people," one of them replied. "There are all kinds of straight people, too."

Living in an openly gay neighborhood with clearly open-minded roommates, you'd think that this would have been a perfect opportunity for me to come out. There was another young comedienne named Ro who occasionally crashed on our couch. One night, after one of my roommates tried to hit on her, Ro confessed that she was gay.

"She was actually afraid that I wouldn't want to be friends with her anymore," my roommate later told me, shaking his head in disbelief. "I mean, I couldn't believe that Rosie (last name: O'Donnell) would even be worried about something like that. It crushed me that she would think it would even matter."

But I understood why she was afraid. At least she had the guts to be honest about it with her friends.

I think it drove me crazy to see so many openly gay people around me, especially the ones who were my age—I secretly admired them for living honestly, while secretly hating them for acting so differently from me.

Eventually it got to be too much. I moved back home with my parents in Valley Forge, a development I found myself explaining one night to Paul Reiser.

Everyone who worked at Comedy Works loved Paul. He was hilarious, a rising star who, despite having just done the movie *Diner*, always hung out with us after his shows, taking a genuine interest in our lives. One night he asked me where I lived.

"With my parents at home," I explained. Paul seemed confused—I still looked a lot older than I was—so I quickly added: "But I'm nineteen. That's where I belong."

Reiser laughed and, like the nervous wreck I am, I kept going. "I used to live on Spruce Street, but, you know, it was hard with all the gay people swarming around. You know Spruce Street."

I'm mortified now by what I felt and said back then. Clearly I was looking for some kind of response. I couldn't have been more pleasantly surprised by the one I got.

"Well," Paul said thoughtfully, "maybe someday we'll evolve enough as a society that they won't have to all live on one street."

CHAPTER 14

BOTTLED UP

Todd makes a friend.

When I was around thirteen, we had a pet parrot. You can train parrots to say just about anything, but the most interesting things are the words and phrases that the bird picks up on its own, a kind of fun-house mirror reflection of the home it lives in. Our bird had two favorites:

"Paul [my dad], do me a favor."

"Maureen [my mom], I'm thirsty."

My aunt Lil was a human being, not a parrot, but at times she seemed a little confused at what separated the two species. "Maureen," Lil said to my mom one day, "you need to give your bird some water. He's really thirsty."

As a thirteen-year-old, this was about the most hilarious thing I'd ever heard. "Why is that so funny?" Lil demanded.

When I stopped rolling on the floor long enough to explain to her that talking birds weren't actually using human cognitive skills to put a sentence together, but mimicking what they've heard people say, Lil got indignant. "Okay, okay!" she said. "It's not that big a deal!"

Even now, as an adult, Lil's reaction to the bird still cracks me up. I like to imagine how the conversation between her and the parrot might have continued if we hadn't enlightened her:

"Paul, do me a favor."

"Has anyone seen Paul? The bird's looking for Paul, Maureen. Do you know where he is? The parrot needs a favor."

"Paul, do me a favor."

"Paul's not here right now . . . My name is Lil. Maybe there's something I can do for you?"

"Paul, do me a favor."

"I'm heading out to the store right now. Is there something you need?"

"Paul, do me a favor."

"I just told you—Paul isn't here."

"Paul, do me a favor."

"Look, I'm trying to help. But you're making it really hard."

"Maureen, I'm thirsty."

"Fine! I'll get you some water . . . What, you don't say thank you?"

"Maureen, I'm thirsty."

"You know, for a bird, you're a real asshole."

Then again, maybe there aren't as many differences between people and parrots as we think. As a teenager, I was surrounded by open-mindedness—people like my parents and Paul

Reiser. But I still felt miles away from being able to talk to any of them about my sexual feelings.

Okay, I'd occasionally admit to myself, *you're gay.* But that was as far as I got. I buried whatever thoughts and feelings I was experiencing as fast as I could. When I look back and wonder why I felt like I had to hide from everyone, one reason stands out above all others: From a very young age I heard the word "gay" used as a pejorative term. The word—along with others like "fairy," "homo," and "fag"—was almost always used to express dislike or distaste, a substitute for "different," "weird," or "out of the ordinary."

"That car is so gay."

"What are you, a homo?"

"Don't be such a faggot."

I don't think that I was being oversensitive—these were the facts, a reasonable conclusion I'd drawn from the environment I grew up in. Every time someone said those words, it felt like a paper cut. The little wounds kept building and building until all I could hear was:

"Gaygayfaggotgaysissygayhomogayfairypansygaygay . . ."

You get the idea. The crazy part, at least with the benefit of hindsight, is that most of the people who were using these words weren't really homophobic, which makes the whole situation feel even more sad. I mean, if you're a full-on homophobe, at least you're speaking in a way that's true to your feelings. But the majority of people—people who never would have consciously meant to hurt me—were using these words in a way that did. The vibe they were sending out to the world didn't match what they were carrying in their hearts. Kind of weird to think that, when it comes to words like these, the homophobe is the one who's doing a better job of articulating his true feelings.

Even though a lot of comedians I was surrounded by were evolved and open-minded, there were plenty who weren't. I heard countless gay jokes told on and off the stage. Eddie Murphy and Andrew Dice Clay made jokes in their specials about homosexuals—sometimes even AIDS—and got big laughs.

As a comedian, you have the right to talk about whatever you want. That's the point of what we do. But at the same time, you can still be judged for what you say, by time, by your peers, or both. Watch those old Eddie Murphy specials now—there's no doubting his comedic genius and abilities, but do you think those gay jokes have really withstood the test of time? There's nothing wrong with getting into topics that are taboo or controversial; the real test is in your approach. Are you going after an easy laugh by perpetuating an old stereotype? Or are you coming at it from a new angle, using comedy as a tool that can shatter the old stereotypes and make people look at a situation in a different way? You don't have to spend money going to a comedy club to hear the same old takes on worn-out stereotypes—that kind of ignorance is easy to find in the real world.

Hearing my friends (and sometimes the people I looked up to) making those kinds of jokes just made me withdraw even more. I figured that as long as I stayed in the closet, those jokes weren't about me. I didn't fit the stereotype. Maybe it's more accurate to say that the stereotype didn't fit me, a relatively straight-acting guy who happened to be attracted to other guys. In fact, I was so sure those jokes weren't about me, I added a bit to my act where I imagined what it would be like to get pulled over by an overly effeminate cop with a lisp. I figured that if I

was really gay and the joke didn't bother me, then it was probably okay for me to use it.

Clearly I was wrong—in hindsight, it's easy to see that I
was guilty of perpetuating the same stereotypes that left me so
confused about my own situation—but in these early stages of
my career, I was still trying to figure out what worked and what
didn't. Fortunately, I was getting plenty of opportunities. Comedy Works was going bananas, pulling in 300 people a night.
Between there and the "one-nighters"—local bars that offered
weekly comedy nights—I was performing several times a week.

I hadn't yet learned that doing good comedy means tapping into the personal, talking about the things in your life that
you're passionate about. God forbid I mention how I liked things
to be perfect or clean—that might give audiences the wrong
(right) idea. Jokes about dating were obviously off the table, because dating wasn't something that I knew anything about.

Man, I was frustrated. I would see guys I was attracted to
and couldn't say a word about it to anyone. *Just focus on the comedy,* I told myself. *You can live without the rest.*

One night, after a show, I was out with some comedians
getting a cheesesteak. I noticed a guy who was looking at me. I
looked back at him. I don't know how I knew, but I *knew*. Or at
least I thought I did.

Nothing was discussed openly. You thought you made a
connection with someone and you hoped you weren't wrong.
"Gaydar" hadn't been invented yet, so most of the time it was
just a waiting game to see who'd make the first move.

By the way, while we're speaking about gaydar—the ability
that some people claim allows them to spot a homosexual from
a mile away—I think the people who say they have it are full

of shit. Everyone's quick to tell you about the time their gaydar "worked," but I can't tell you how many people have bragged about their gaydar to me who had no idea that I was gay. *Really?* I'd think to myself. *You picking anything up right now? I bet yours needs new batteries. That's the problem . . .*

Back to the cheesesteak: When my friends got up to go, I told them that I was going to walk back to my car. Instead, I just sat there for another half hour, making eye contact with the guy.

He seemed normal. A regular guy. Not overly tough, not overly feminine. I remember thinking, *This guy can't be gay.*

Eventually, one of us spoke. "How ya doin'?"

"Good . . . How are you doin'?"

We made small talk for maybe another half hour before he offered to drive me back to my car. If he had been more direct, it probably would have turned me off. He would have seemed too comfortable. But the longer we sat there, feeling nervous, the more I was attracted to him. His hand somehow found its way to my knee. That was it—just a quick touch, then he took it away.

"Sorry. Did that make you uncomfortable?" he asked.

"No," I said. "Are you, uh . . ." I couldn't even say the word.

"Are you?" he asked.

The floodgates opened. While we ended up fooling around a little, mostly we just talked. I couldn't believe I'd met someone who seemed just like me. We talked about how disconnected and uncomfortable we felt. He told me about a guy he knew who had actually come out to his parents, which sounded fucking insane—we were both hell-bent on taking our secret to our deaths. Our perfect fantasy lives involved getting married to women who developed cancer and died young and tragically. "Poor guy," people would say thirty years later. "He never got over Karen . . ."

We sat at a diner until the sun rose, stumbling out into the sunlight with no place to go. We traded numbers—when I wrote his down in my address book, I was so paranoid that I changed a couple of digits so nobody would . . . No, it still doesn't make any fucking sense.

We met and fooled around a few more times after that. I didn't feel dirty afterward; I felt great. There was someone else out there who was like me, who made me feel normal. I wanted to share my good feelings with everyone I knew.

But besides him, who was I going to tell?

To be honest, I couldn't really tell him, either. Saying anything out loud would make it seem real and no one was ready for that. So one night when we were at Denny's and he started flirting with girls, I simply took it as a sign that he was no longer interested. I'm sure if I had asked him about it we could have talked and helped one another to figure things out, but I didn't and we didn't. We never did anything after that. I'd gone for years hiding my sexuality from everyone who was straight—now I had a new friend who was gay and I had to hide from him, too.

This wasn't going in the right direction.

CHAPTER 15
NO-SHOW GEORGE

Theater in the round.

The Valley Forge Music Fair was a three-thousand-seat theater-in-the-round with a stage that actually rotated to give everyone in the audience a better view. I'd occasionally worked there in high school as a parking attendant and an usher. My regular gig at Comedy Works—not to mention the money I was saving by living at home—meant I didn't have to park cars anymore, but I used to run into one of the managers around town, a guy named Jim. "So you're a comedian now," he'd say. "When are you going to bring your act to Valley Forge?"

"Not yet!" I'd reply. I knew that I wasn't ready. Or at least I didn't think I was, until I got another phone call from Steve Young. "How would you like to open for George Jones at the Valley Forge Music Fair?"

At first I thought he was joking. So did my former cowork-ers when they saw me at the theater and asked what I was doing.

"I'm the opening act for George Jones," I said.

"Shut the fuck up!" they replied.

I arrived at the venue four hours early, chewing on a couple of pills my mother gave me to keep my stomach from twisting in knots. I was about to perform for ten minutes in front of the biggest crowd I'd ever faced. Ten minutes of material was all I had, and only seven of them were any good.

I paced around backstage. Jim walked over and patted me on the shoulders. "It's going to be fun!" he said. "You'll do, like, ten or fifteen minutes . . . It'll be great!"

"Fifteen minutes?" I repeated, trying to sound sure of my-self.

"Sure! Just have fun with it," Jim said cheerfully. He thought he was doing me a favor.

I dug around in my brain for anything that could fill more time. A few minutes later, Jim came back around and delivered another blow to my confidence.

"You *might* have to do twenty."

I was speechless.

"We'll see," he added. "Hopefully he won't be 'No-Show George' tonight . . ."

That's his nickname? Are you fucking shitting me? First it's fif-teen minutes, then maybe twenty, and now he might not even show up at all?

". . . We'll put you on once we know he's en route from the hotel. It's all going to be great."

What the hell am I going to do? I could get the audience to sing the theme to The Brady Bunch *with me . . . That might take up three minutes, especially if I tell them they did a shitty job the first time. And there's always crowd work . . ."*

Crowd work—improvised interactions with specific members of the audience—is a great way to stretch for time if you don't have enough material. It's not hard to do and most crowds will enjoy it.

Save your material, I told myself as I stepped onto the stage. I think I told one joke from my prepared set before shifting my focus to the audience.

Which would have been fine, had I been dealing with a crowd that was sitting in one place. I'd completely forgotten to account for the rotating stage—by the time I came up with a joke, I'd lost sight of whatever audience members I'd been interacting with.

"Where is that couple from Florida?" I asked, scanning the crowd for two people I talked to a few seconds earlier. "We're over here!" I heard from somewhere behind me, forcing me to turn around in order to deliver the joke. I repeated the bit over and over again, twisting and turning, struggling to make it work.

But despite my panic (or maybe because of it) the crowd had a good time. Thirty seconds into the set, I knew I was killing. By the time No-Show George arrived twenty-five minutes later, Jim almost had to drag me off of the stage.

I ducked into the underground tunnel that led back to the greenroom, where George Jones was preparing to go on. George was friendly and we exchanged a few words, but one thing he said stood out above all others. "How is the crowd?" he asked.

How is the crowd? I thought. *Why do you care what the crowd is like? You're George Jones. They came to see you!* I couldn't believe that someone that famous would still care what the crowd is like. I wondered if you ever stopped caring.

I didn't have to wonder very long. Later that year, I opened for George Benson, Luther Vandross, Tammy Wynette, and the Temptations. All of them asked me the same question when I came offstage: How is the crowd?

I guess you never stop caring.

CHAPTER 16

THE PERFECT ROOM

Todd goes to Broadway.

About eight months later, I got another call from Steve Young: "How would you like to open for Patti La-Belle? She's doing a month and a half at the Minskoff Theatre on Broadway and she wants you to be her opening act."

I was excited. I didn't know a whole lot about Patti LaBelle, but I knew what Broadway was. "Of course I will. Not that it matters, but what do I get paid?"

Steve laughed. "I'm going to be honest with you. When they asked me how much, I told them one thousand dollars. Thinking *per week*. Well, they came back and told me a thousand a show sounded fine."

"A thousand a show? How many shows?"

"Seven or eight a week."

For a kid with a severe learning disability who had never understood math, I managed to do the arithmetic pretty fucking fast: I was rich! Seven grand a week is a lot of money for an adult today, but in the '80s, for a kid with no bills or expenses, this was like striking gold. Of course I burned through that money like Richard Pryor in *Brewster's Millions*. I bought dinners and picked up bar tabs, threw catered parties at my parents' house, rented a new apartment, and spent $4,000 fixing it up. If Suze Orman saw how careless I was back then she would have had a heart attack long before I did.

But I didn't care. Why would I? I thought this was going to be my life from now on.

Every Sunday, after the matinee show, a limo would drive me back to my parents' house. Sometimes Patti's son Zuri would catch a ride as well. He was about thirteen—more or less my mental age—so we found plenty of common ground, laughing and doing bits along the way. Sometimes we'd pretend to fight over a seat. "I'm her opening act, so I should be able to pick where I want to sit," I'd say.

"But I'm her son. Son is more important than opening act!"

I could tell Zuri understood my sense of humor and it wasn't hard to figure out why: Patti had a great sense of humor, too.

At every performance, when she sang "Lady Marmalade," Patti invited people from the audience to dance with her onstage. One night, her backup singers thought it would be funny if I joined them—wearing the same sparkly, sequined dress they wore. I stood on the wings in the dress, fighting my nerves and second-guessing the decision. "What if she doesn't think it's funny?" I asked one of the singers who peeked backstage to see if I was ready.

"Oh, trust me, she will." Before I had a chance to offer a rebuttal she literally pushed me onto the stage.

Panic spread throughout my entire body. If Patti didn't laugh, I was going to be fired for sure. Luckily for me, she cracked up the moment she saw me. "Folks, I did not know about this!" she said, as soon as she could breathe again. Patti turned to her backup singers. "Girls, you're just jealous that he looks better in that dress than you do!" She brought me front and center and we danced for a few seconds, bringing the audience in on the joke. Patti was a great dancer. I remember thinking how amazing it was that she was able to move like that at her age. (Her age, of course, being only forty.)

Every night, when I was done with my set and she was about to start hers, Patti stopped by my greenroom to say a few kind words (and yes, sometimes to ask me how the crowd was). These greenroom visits were so routine that I never thought of them as a big deal—until I mentioned them to my family.

"Shut the fuck up, Todd!" Corey said incredulously.

"I'm telling you, she comes by every day and we hang out." No one believed me, but since they were all coming to a show soon, I figured I'd let them see for themselves.

The night of the show arrived. I'd done my set and was sitting in the greenroom with my brothers, waiting for Patti's visit. "You'll see," I promised. "She'll stop by in a second . . ."

Just like clockwork, Patti turned the corner and . . . walked right past the door without saying a single word.

I'm not sure that I've ever been more embarrassed. *How could this be? The one time I really need her to drop in, she decides not to?*

I tried to come up with an excuse—any excuse that might

sound reasonable. But before I could open my mouth, Patti turned around and walked into the room. "I'm sorry, guys, I just can't do that to Todd!" Somehow my brothers had gotten to her before the show and put her up to it.

Sometimes we would hang out after the show. Patti took me to restaurants or to see other musical acts that she enjoyed. I blame my obsession with "the perfect room" on one of these outings.

I am obsessed with the perfect room. (A serious, crazy obsession, as certain club owners might tell you.) A room that's perfectly lit, with the right-sized stage and the right-sized audience—not too big, not too small, but intimate enough to be great. I know that this room exists because I saw it once in 1984.

Patti took me to a club where a friend of hers was playing. Unlike the Minskoff, which had 2,500 seats, this place only had room for 125. Electric candles sat on top of tables covered in black cloth. The maître d' escorted us to our table through an elegantly dressed audience, using a flashlight to see where he was going.

A small walkway lined with lightbulbs led from the tables to a tiny stage. As the houselights dimmed, the band quietly took their positions, wearing suits that were so well fitted they might as well have been painted on. From somewhere in the room, an announcer with the deepest voice I've ever heard exclaimed: "Ladies and gentlemen, good evening and welcome to a night with Sarah Dash!"

The band let out a two-count with a thump of the drums. When the second drumstick came down, every candle in the house went out, leaving only the barely lit stage. Another heavy thump of the drums and all the lights on the stage went out, leaving only a single candle on top of the piano. "It's showtime!" With another heavy drumbeat, the piano player leaned in and blew out the candle. The room was now completely dark—I mean pitch black. The audience sat there in anticipation for at least ten seconds before the announcer said the words everyone was waiting for: "Sarah Dash!"

A single spotlight hit the back of the room where she was standing. The maître d' guided her to the stage. The band played a soft and steady beat that came to an abrupt stop as she turned to face the crowd. "LET'S DO THIS!" she screamed.

The band took off like a missile. The energy built and built for the entire show. Everyone in the room knew they were participating in something special.

Ever since then, I've been on a quest to re-create that feeling at a comedy show. If you're one of the club owners I've been driving up a wall for the last twenty years, I've only got one thing to say: Blame it on Patti LaBelle.

But when I think of Patti, the memory that stands out most was the night my parents came to see me open the show. Every performer dreams of succeeding in front of his or her parents; thanks to Patti, I got to do it on Broadway before I was twenty. When Patti found out they were in the audience, she extended a level of kindness that went far above and beyond what any opening act could ever hope for. She shined a spotlight on my mom and dad and introduced them to the applauding crowd. "I'd like to dedicate this next song to Todd," she said, then launched into "There's a Winner in You."

This was, I imagine, comforting to my parents in a way that went beyond pride. A couple of years earlier they were worrying about what I was going to do with the rest of my life. About what was going to happen to a kid who had failed almost every single grade. I think that night they were able to experience some peace of mind: I was going to be okay.

It was a moment that became even more poignant when my dad died a short time later.

I watched Patti give, no bullshit, 100 percent of herself at every single show. She had a way of interacting with the crowd that always felt real. Even though she was a singer and I was a comedian, she taught me everything I needed to know about respecting the audience.

I've done a lot of cool things in my career since then, but nothing has impacted me more than the six weeks I spent with Patti. I've always wanted to let her know how much the experience meant to me. There's a poem—I think it's by Ralph Waldo Emerson—that perfectly captures my feelings. I've thought many times about sending it to her, but I always wimp out, thinking, *She's Patti LaBelle and she probably gets letters like this all of the time.* If, by some small chance, you're reading this book, Patti, this is for you:

> To laugh often and love much. To win the respect of intelligent persons, and the affection of children. To know that even one life has breathed easier because you have lived—This is to have succeeded.

CHAPTER 17
SMOKEY JOE'S

Todd discovers a friendly bar.

When I got back to Philadelphia, the city felt like a ghost town. My friends had all graduated school and gone on to college, where they were partying and growing up and doing all the things that college kids get to do. I wasn't jealous—I mean, I was playing Broadway, right? Okay, maybe I was a little jealous. Not having them around meant a huge void in my social life. I knew that if I wanted to continue to grow, not just as a comedian but as a human being, I needed something more than stand-up. I had to get out of my comfort zone and make some new friends and experiences to talk about.

A few of my friends came home that summer. One night we decided to go to Smokey Joe's, a popular bar on the Main Line. I didn't bother to bring my ID, because I already looked thirty and hadn't been carded since the ninth grade. Except this time. While my friends got to go inside, I had to drive all the way home to retrieve my license.

When I got back an hour and a half later, there was a different guy at the door. His name was Jimmy Ryan, and he was one of the owner's sons. "Hey . . . I've seen you before," he said. "You do stand-up comedy, right?"

"Yeah."

"That's great! Come on in!"

On the one hand, I was happy to be recognized, but the feeling was soured by the fact that, had Jimmy been there earlier, it would have saved me the drive (and made me look really cool in front of my friends). But his bar was awesome and, later that night, I told him so.

"We hang out here almost every night, after hours," he said. "If you ever want to come by, just knock on the side door."

One night, after doing a couple of shows at Comedy Works, I decided to stop by Smokey Joe's to see if what Jimmy said was true. I knocked on the side door. Sure enough, around ten or fifteen people, mostly employees, were sitting around a fireplace, drinking and having fun.

Smokey Joe's quickly became a substitute for my college experience. I found myself surrounded by people my age who all came from different backgrounds and were always up for a late-night laugh. I bonded with everyone I met there and still keep in touch with most of them to this day.

I got to know the friendly bartender, even if I never could remember his name. (All I knew was that it was something rich-sounding—"Harrison!" everyone would always remind me.) We got drunk and did stupid things, like the night Jimmy handed out shot glasses, which we downed and smashed against a brick wall. We got drunk and did *really* stupid things, like the night I tried the same trick with an empty vodka bottle, forgetting for a critical moment that I sucked at sports, and missed the brick wall, throwing the bottle through the plate glass window at the front of the bar.

As soon as it left my hand I knew I fucked up. The giant window shattered, spilling broken glass into the street. Everyone fell silent. I was devastated. We were having such a great time and I was the asshole who took it too far. I'm the guy who got sloppy and now they're all going to have to answer for this. "I'm so sorry," was the best I could think of to say to Jimmy.

He must have seen how badly I felt by the expression on my face. "Todd, I don't care. I swear."

It was sweet of him to say, but I knew he didn't mean it. I just threw a fucking bottle through the front window of his father's bar.

"It's really okay," he insisted. "Want me to prove it to you?" And with that he swiped every glass and bottle still on the bar onto the floor. Most of them broke on impact. I hate to admit it, but it worked: Just like that, we were all laughing again.

The next morning, Jimmy told his father that someone had driven by and thrown something through the window. "That makes total sense, Jimmy," said his dad, a twenty-year veteran of the bar business. "It's just that all the glass is broken on the *outside*."

But there was a new window in place by the end of the day. No one ever panicked or got mad at Smokey Joe's and the place ran like a well-oiled machine. It was fun to be a part of it.

CHAPTER 18

FAKING IT

Todd finds a soul mate. (Almost.)

So there was still that one pesky problem, the one I had started referring to (in my own mind) as my *situation*.

It was inevitable that my new group of friends at Smokey Joe's would have questions about my personal life, so I came up with a plan: I picked the hottest girl who came to the bar—a girl who was so hot that even I knew she was hot—and told everyone I had a crush on her. "Fuck!" I'd say like I was trying to pull out a splinter. "She's way out of my league."

Good plan, right? Sure, until the night my friend Mick walked over to me and said, "Todd, you know that girl you have a crush on? Well, guess who wants to talk to you?"

Now, reader, I want you to picture a twelve-year-old kid whose voice is cracking from puberty when I say that I replied,

"Oh . . . Great . . . Awesome . . . Good news!" *Are you fucking shitting me?* I thought. *I picked the hottest girl in the bar and then ignored her night after night. Why the hell would she want to talk to me?* (Of course, that's how little I knew about women.)

It only got worse when she walked over and started talking to me. It was time for Plan B, a strategy that I've used many times since to avoid certain awkward situations: I drank. A lot. It was basically a race to see if I could get drunk enough to black out. I'm not saying it was healthy and I'm certainly not proud of it, but most of the time it worked. As an added bonus, sometimes I'd hear a story the next day about how I was hanging all over some chick the night before. I was sure it never went anywhere—pretty sure, anyway—but I was happy for everyone else to draw their own conclusions about what happened.

Sometimes I got really lucky, like the night a girl at the bar told everyone that she spent the night with me. "You never hooked up with her, did you?" Mick asked.

"Who?" I replied, checking to see if she was cute before I (fake) confessed. I mean, come on—at this point I had a (fake) reputation to uphold. I had (fake) standards. "Well . . . maybe. I don't kiss and tell."

I couldn't believe how fortunate I was—if this girl wanted everyone to think that we were fucking, I should have been paying her. In that moment she was like a saint to me.

Here's a funny thing about being gay: It doesn't leave a mark, not one that you can see, anyway. When you're black, people tend to go out of their way not to say anything around you that could even remotely be construed as racist. But nobody knew that I was gay. I was like a secret agent, privy to all kinds of conversations where people would say what they really thought without any fear of offending me.

I remember one night at Comedy Works, as the AIDS scare was growing, there was a debate over whether or not you'd feel comfortable drinking from the same glass as a gay person. "I don't think you can even get it that way," someone said.

"But I still wouldn't do it, would you?" someone else asked.

That conversation alone probably threw me back ten years in terms of becoming open about my sexuality.

As funny as my efforts to hide might seem in retrospect, at the time, I really, really wanted to be straight. Maybe there was still time to change. But how? I couldn't walk into the library and get a book on the subject (or even read that book if I found one). How would I even ask? "Hi! Do you have anything on not being . . . I think that I'm . . . I've got this *situation* on my hands . . ."

So I improvised: I would still think of guys when I *started* masturbating, only now, in an effort to change millions of years of evolution, I would force myself to think of women when I finished.

Needless to say, it didn't help me become any less gay, although I did masturbate a lot less often.

Blacking out drunk, lying about sexual partners, and forcing myself to have straight thoughts helped me get through my day. But none of that prepared me for the complications that arose when I met someone who felt like my soul mate, a person who could understand me on every level. There was only one problem:

She was a girl.

Katy was a regular at Smokey Joe's. From the moment I met her, I loved everything about her. We had the same sense of humor. We liked the same things. I started to crave her company. I didn't care what we did, as long as we were together. If she had errands to run, I'd come along and hang out all day while she drove around the city. Sometimes we would get sandwiches and just sit in the car, people-watching and talking about everything. (Or *almost* everything.)

Once we even pretended we were married.

Comedians often get hired to do corporate events. It's kind of like working a comedy club, except that instead of playing to an intimate room full of people waiting to be entertained, you're in a some hotel banquet hall in front of four hundred IBM employees who aren't necessarily there to laugh. Corporate events are also different from the clubs in that they pay really, really well, which is the reason why you do them.

For my first corporate event, a company Christmas party, the hosts added an extra layer of difficulty—someone had the brilliant idea that, instead of introducing me as a comic, I would pretend to be the new corporate VP. I figured it was better if I didn't tell them that I was barely literate and had failed to graduate high school. It's not like they were totally forthcoming with me, either: No one at the company had bothered to tell me that the old corporate VP I was supposedly replacing had been fired and that several in-house employees had been passed over for promotion. To put it mildly, there was probably a little animosity toward the twenty-three-year-old kid eating dinner at the president's table.

I brought Katy with me for moral support, telling everyone that she was my girlfriend. We might have been young, stupid, and totally clueless about the company I was supposedly working for, but we figured that as long as we stayed at the table and didn't talk to anyone, we could probably pull it off.

But being young and stupid, we inevitably decided to leave the safety of the table for the bar, where we downed a few shots. "I'm feeling a little nervous," I whispered in Katy's ear.

Three women—our new pretend coworkers—immediately turned their attention to us. "So what are you two whispering about?" one of them asked.

I started to sweat, fumbling for a response. I hadn't counted on Katy being even more nervous than I was, so I might have done a literal spit-take when she replied:

"I'm pregnant."

What the fuck?! Talk about an overreaction. Everyone's eyes seemed to gravitate toward the empty shot glasses on the bar. "It's okay!" I said quickly. "We were going to get married anyway."

I should mention here that while I was twenty-three, I probably looked like I was about thirty. And that Katy, who was about the same age as me, looked like she was maybe nineteen. I was trying to drag her back to the president's table, the sanctuary we never should have left in the first place, when I heard the PA go on: "Ladies and gentlemen, please welcome our new vice president, Todd Glass!"

As I stepped up to the microphone, I could see the three women we met at the bar whispering to their coworkers, spreading the word, no doubt, about the new thirty-year-old VP who'd knocked up his teenage girlfriend. It's bad enough playing to an audience that isn't looking for comedy—this group was glaring at me with hatred in their eyes. I wanted to launch into my routine, but I knew I wasn't supposed to break character yet. I scrambled to improvise.

"Look," I said. "I get it that no one here is a big fan of mine right now. I'm sorry. Maybe there's something we can do that will bring us all closer together. Do you guys know how to sing the theme to *The Brady Bunch*?"

If you happen to be a real corporate executive, you might want to take note: Everyone loves to sing. The hard part is finding a song that everyone knows the words to. But in those days, everybody knew the words to *The Brady Bunch*. Within seconds I had the whole room laughing and singing along. I'm sure I would have been the world's shittiest VP, but tonight I'd won over the crowd. "I know this is going to be a fun year," I finished. "Thank you!"

The president took the stage and—finally—told everyone that I was a comedian. I took the microphone back and shared the story with the group. "You guys ever watch *Three's Company*?" I asked. "The situations you see on *Three's Company* don't happen in real life. But tonight they just did."

The irony is that my real life was playing out like *Three's Company* in reverse. That show mined a lot of humor out of a protagonist who, in order to live in an apartment with two beautiful women, had to pretend that he was gay. I would often stay over at Katy's house, pretending that I was straight.

Nothing was *happening*, of course. I wanted to tell her so badly that I was gay, that the reason I wasn't putting any moves on her had nothing to do with the way she looked or her personality. But I was still years away from even being able to consider that kind of honesty.

"Todd's shy around girls," my mother told her. "Maybe you should be a little more aggressive." My mom—who was just trying to be helpful—even offered to help me buy a wedding ring.

Being straight was turning out to be a lot harder than I thought.

CHAPTER 19
TWO PIECES OF ADVICE

Todd gets some wisdom from a comedian he looks up to.

I was working as much as I could. Steve Young had me at Comedy Works almost every weekend. Andy Scarpati, the owner of six or seven smaller clubs in Philadelphia, New Jersey, and Delaware, also gave me a lot of work.

One weekend, Jay Leno returned to Comedy Works. We were shooting the shit after the show, and someone asked him if he'd ever seen an act that was so good he didn't want to follow it.

"Well, there is actually one guy, his name is Dennis Miller. When he connects with the audience, man, you don't want to be the guy going on after him."

Steve hired Dennis a few weeks later, and everything Jay told us made sense—Dennis was on that night and absolutely annihilated. Pretty soon he was a regular sight at Comedy

Works, and I got to spend a lot of time hanging out with him.

One night, we were walking down Chestnut Street after a show. I made some joke about Philadelphia being the hotbed of comedy.

"If you want to make it in this business," Dennis said, "eventually you gotta go to New York or L.A."

I knew he was right. "But there are so many comedians in those cities," I replied. "It seems like it would be overwhelming. Just another comedian moving to the coast."

"Don't do that," Dennis said. "There are a lot of people doing everything. There are a lot of carpenters in the world, too. But if you do what you do well, and you give it everything you've got, you'll be the carpenter who does well."

That was the second-best piece of advice that Dennis Miller ever gave me. The best came a few months later. We were hanging out at a bar after a show and I'd just made some offhanded comment that got him laughing.

"This," he said to me, "is what's funny about you. What the hell are you doing up there onstage?"

While it might have sounded like criticism, I could see the compliment. Nothing is more exciting for a comedian than to make other comedians laugh, especially if it's someone whose work you respect and admire. I'd been so focused on creating a polished act, I wasn't letting my real personality come out. Dennis's comment was only bad news if I didn't take it to heart. I wasn't about to trash my entire act, but I started using open mike nights as an opportunity to try out different angles, looking for something that felt more authentic to who I was.

Before moving on to the next chapter, let's take a second to stop and sit with the irony in that statement.

Okay, that's enough. You can turn the page now.

CHAPTER 20
LEAVING PHILADELPHIA

Some funny (and not so funny) things happen on the way to Los Angeles.

Some nights, after partying at Smokey Joe's, I'd crash on Harrison's couch—Harrison, the bartender with the rich-sounding name, lived in a house with my friends Mick and John. After one stretch where I'd slept there for about three months straight, Harrison suggested that it might be easier for me to move in.

It was around this time when Steve Young told me that he was moving to Los Angeles to pursue a writing career. Lots of people, including Steve, thought it was time for me to make a similar move. I started talking about L.A. to anyone who would listen.

The topic came up one night with my friend Caroline Jones and her parents, who were in town from California to visit her at Villanova. "You could always come and live with us for a while," suggested Randy, her father. It was a nice thing to say, I thought, even if he really didn't mean it.

There were a few things I had to do before I could even think about moving. The first issue was cash: The move would cost a lot of money and I had none. Somehow all that Patti La-Belle cash was gone (shocker) and I was almost dead broke.

There was a waitress at Comedy Works who got a speeding ticket on the way to work. I mentioned it during my act, even passing around a hat to help her pay for it. By the time the hat got back to me, she'd made enough to cover the ticket and then some.

Which gave me an idea: "I'm thinking about moving to Los Angeles!" I announced a few nights later. The hat went around the room again, returning to me with a couple of hundred dollars. I felt like the smartest guy in the world until I got a call from Steve.

"You can't do that, Todd."

"Why not?"

"Because you're taking advantage of the audience."

I didn't like it, but knew he was right. We used the money to send flowers to a waitress who was in the hospital.

As the end of the year approached—despite having almost no money and no idea where I was going to live—I really felt like I was ready to go. But plans don't always work out the way you want them to. One night a policeman knocked on the door to Harrison's house. "Is Todd Glass here?" he asked.

"I'm Todd Glass."

"We've been trying to call you, but there seems to be a problem with your phone." There was a problem with our phone—it had been disconnected for lack of payment. The cop continued: "Your father is at Paoli Hospital."

My dad had been driving on the highway when he began to feel ill. He pulled over to the side of the road and threw up. A passerby saw him lying by the side of the road, wisely recognized that my father was having a heart attack, and tried to give him CPR.

When I arrived at the hospital, the rest of my family greeted me with the news: my dad was dead. I let out something that sounded like a cross between a pained whimper and a primal scream. I turned and punched the wall.

But suddenly a peaceful calm settled over me. "We're going to be okay," I said to my family. "We're all going to be okay. We're going to have Christmas, and it's going to be okay."

A nurse asked us if we wanted to say good-bye to him. My younger brother, Corey, and I went in together. The room was cold and still. Dad's body was on the table. A few moments passed in silence before I quietly said:

"Should we check his pockets for money?"

For a second, I wasn't sure I'd said the right thing. But I got a great laugh out of Corey. It sounds so cliché, but you've got to have a sense of humor about this kind of stuff. If all you're doing is making jokes, you're probably not dealing with death very well. But if you're just crying, that's not the best thing either. Later, back at my parents' house, my brothers and I mock-argued over my dad's clothes, getting into a tugging match over a shirt that ended with the shirt being torn in half. We fell on the floor laughing. But later that night, I heard Michael throwing up in the bathroom, literally sick with grief.

Here's another cliché that's true: If you've got something nice to say about people, tell them while they're still alive. My mind raced back to a conversation I'd had a month earlier with one of my dad's employees. My father could be gruff on the outside: I remember once when my friend Doug Doyle insisted on addressing him in an overly deferential way—"Nice to meet you, Mr. Glass . . . Can I get something for you, Mr. Glass?"—finally leading my dad to say, "Hey, son, fucking relax . . . What are you looking for, a handout?" But my dad was also one of the most open-minded and nonjudgmental people I've ever met. I described him to the employee as a cross between Ed Asner and Phil Donahue.

When the employee told my dad what I'd said, I was upset. "Why did you tell him that?" I said to her. "I can't believe you told him I said that!"

But now, seeing my dad on the table, I couldn't have been gladder that she did. I leaned down and whispered in his ear. "You did a good job."

About fifty people came to a service at our house, including a lot of my friends from Smokey Joe's. We were used to hanging out and laughing and having fun. We'd never been around each other in a situation like this one. It was uncomfortable. No one knew what to say or how to act. But luckily we still had our twisted sense of humor. At one point during the service, my friend John slowly leaned in toward me, pointed to the yarmulke on my head, and whispered, "Jew!"

I thought that was about the funniest thing I'd ever heard.

The rabbi who married my parents and presided over my bar mitzvah gave a great speech. "We have a lot of different kinds of people in this room," he began, "and I don't know what everybody's beliefs are. Some people think, we do this, we go there. Some people don't know what to think. Some don't think about it at all. But I can tell you something that's a fact, something that we can all agree on no matter what our backgrounds are: He's not in pain. And our memories are real. Now obviously, we miss his presence, and that can't be replaced. But he's not in pain and the memories are real. We can find comfort in that."

I still find comfort in the memories. I have an old sweater of my dad's. Even if it doesn't smell like him anymore, I still have a good cry every time I pull it out. But I can't help but wonder what our relationship could have been. I think he would have loved the comedy. Given how accepting he'd always been—toward his family, his friends, and his employees—I really think that he would have been okay with me being gay. Circle this cliché in red: Soak in the people you love while they're still here.

After the memorial service, my sister-in-law Meryl approached me with a look that managed to be both concerned and adorable. "Is it okay to say happy birthday?" she asked. Obviously my twenty-third birthday didn't seem that important on this particular day. But I appreciated the gesture and gave her a big hug.

As I'm writing this book, it's forced me to recognize some of the times that might otherwise have drifted past, times when people have acted kindly toward me in ways that were completely unexpected. A few days later, I got a phone call. "Todd, this is Randy Jones . . . Caroline's dad?"

"Sure, I remember," I said. "How are you?"

"Actually, I'm a little upset. I told you that you could come stay with us in L.A. What's the matter, our house isn't good enough for you?

I felt a sudden burst of excitement. *If he's calling me on the phone, he must really mean it!* I still didn't have any money, but now I knew I had a friendly place to stay. My fears about Los Angeles all but disappeared. I was finally ready to make my move.

CHAPTER 21
THE COMEDY STORE

Los Angeles!

For most twenty-three-year-olds with a car, a cross-country move means one thing: road trip!

Only I wasn't most twenty-three-year-olds. Driving long distance would require reading road signs, following directions, and, most of all, using maps. As you can probably guess by now, I was incapable of doing any of that, especially the part with the maps.

I remember the first time a history teacher pulled down a map of the United States. Just looking at it made me dizzy—all those lines and names! How could anyone in their right mind ever learn all that? It's still hard to admit some of this stuff sometimes, like when someone gives me directions: "Just get off the freeway and head south."

"Is that a right or a left?"

"I'm not sure . . . It's south."

"I don't carry a fucking compass with me! Right or left?"

It can get really bad at hotels, where desk clerks love to draw directions on their stupid little maps. I panic as soon as I see them reaching under the desk. *No no no! Please don't draw me a map! Just tell me the first two steps and, when I get there, I'll ask someone else how to go the rest of the way.*

So a road trip was out of the question. Fortunately, my brother Corey volunteered to drive my car across the country with all of my stuff in it. I went to the airport with Harrison, Mick, and Katy. It was bittersweet—for the last few years I'd spent a lot of days and nights with these people—but when I looked at Katy, I felt guilty. There was so much I wish I could have explained to her.

A few hours later I landed in Burbank, California. I felt like I was exiting the plane into a giant indoor swimming pool where the temperature was a perfectly maintained seventy-two degrees.

This is where I'm going to live.

I took a cab to Steve Young's house, where I crashed for a couple of nights until Corey arrived with my Jeep. (God, do I miss the days when I could fit everything I owned into a Jeep.) Then it was off to the Joneses.

I was scared to drive in California. I'd grown up watching CHiPs—the classic show about how L.A. needed its own special cops just to deal with the highways—and I felt like I was stepping into the insane world I'd seen on TV. The Joneses lived about forty-five minutes south of downtown in a place called Anaheim Hills, so I white-knuckled it until I was sure I'd found the exit.

None of the houses I'd seen in California up to that point were built on spacious lots—even in the expensive areas, it felt like there were fewer than ten feet between you and your neighbor. But the Joneses lived on a huge property that you had to enter through gates. I pressed the buzzer and the gates opened—pretty spectacular, even if it lacked the Nalibotsky touch.

The best thing about the Joneses' house, however, was the Joneses. They couldn't have been any kinder to me. Randy and his wife, Sue, had set up a bedroom for me downstairs, including a brand-new desk.

"I thought you'd need a desk to write your jokes and work on your act," Randy said.

I don't typically (and by "typically," I mean "ever") work on my act at a desk, but I was really moved by their generosity toward a kid who they barely knew.

Steve Young was also a huge help. Besides letting me crash at his place while I waited for my car, he forgave a couple of thousand dollars he'd earned as commission for shows he'd booked for me in Philadelphia. Steve also arranged for me to have an audition for Mitzi Shore, the owner of the legendary Comedy Store.

In 1989, the Comedy Store was the place to be. It was an all-black building sitting on the most exciting part of the Sunset Strip. The outside walls were covered with the names of comedians who performed there, names like Robin Williams, David Letterman, Sam Kinison, and Richard Pryor. The list included Tom Wilson, who remembered me from Comedy Works and offered to put in a good word with Mitzi.

But my confidence started to slip as soon as I entered the

building. Walking up and down the stairs connecting the three packed showrooms felt surreal. This was organized chaos that smelled of rock and roll and comedy history.

I was still struggling to take it all in when Steve nudged me: I was up next, part of a showcase of comedians eager to impress Mitzi. If you succeeded, you got "spots." It might only be one spot a week, it might be six—obviously I was hoping for something like six. If you failed? Thanks for coming. Maybe you can try again in a year or so. All of the names I'd seen on the wall had, at one point or another, stood where I stood now, putting their hopes and dreams in Mitzi's hands.

Mitzi sat in the back of the room . . . At least I think she did. I never saw her that night. Come to think of it, in my thirty-year comedy career I don't think I've ever seen Mitzi Shore. Maybe she doesn't exist. The next morning Steve called to tell me that Mitzi had passed on my act.

I was devastated. I thought of ways I could get on Mitzi's good side. Maybe I could slash one of her tires and then "accidentally" walk by and help her fix it. "So what do you do?" I'd say, catching her in a moment of total appreciation for me. "You own a comedy club? No way! Guess what? I'm a comedian!"

Nowadays, there are all kinds of ways to become a comedian. You can shoot your own videos and put them on the web. Do your own podcast and promote it with social media. There are any number of niche networks of clubs and venues to help you get started.

But back then, if you didn't succeed at the Comedy Store, well, *fuck.*

CHAPTER 22
THE
IMPROV

Todd finds a new comedy home.

The original Improvisation started in New York in 1963. Budd Friedman, an aspiring Broadway producer looking for a way to make some part-time cash, opened a coffeehouse where performers could feel comfortable hanging out after their shows, eating, drinking, and singing with their friends. About a year in, he got a liquor license, a development that, according to Budd, encouraged the comedians to start dropping by. Before long the Improvisation was hosting live comedy on a nightly basis, putting on greats like George Burns, Milton Berle, and George Carlin alongside young comics looking to break in—Jerry Seinfeld, Lily Tomlin, Andy Kaufman, and Jay Leno, to name a few.

As stand-up comedy became more popular in the 1970s,

Budd left a guy named Chris Albrecht to run the New York club and opened a second in Los Angeles.

Budd was (and is) a very creative person. He's always impeccably groomed, wearing expensively tailored suits with tennis shoes and an honest-to-God monocle. He can also be brutally honest in the way that he talks, getting right to the point with the kinds of thoughts that most people would keep to themselves. One story had him standing in the hallway when a comedian wearing a wife-beater tank top walked by. "Hey, Budd! I'm on next," he said. "You should watch my set!"

Budd took one look at the guy and his T-shirt, lowered his monocle, and snapped back: "Muscles aren't funny."

The L.A. Improv had always played second banana to the Comedy Store, but it was growing in popularity thanks to a cable TV show, *An Evening at the Improv,* where comics did their acts in front of the iconic brick wall. I recognized the building from TV as soon as we pulled up to the front. Steve sensed my excitement and reminded me not to get my hopes up. He knew I was still upset about the Comedy Store and didn't want to set me up for another disappointment.

I also recognized Budd from the TV show, but that didn't prepare me for meeting him in person. "Todd, how *are* you? It's so good to meet you." If you're old enough to remember *Gilligan's Island*, think Thurston Howell, and you'll get a sense of Budd's drawl.

I was even more nervous than I'd been for Mitzi—I felt like this was basically my last chance to make it in L.A. The set went well, but I thought the set at the Comedy Store had gone well and that didn't work out. When I was done onstage I made a beeline for the door and slipped outside for a cigarette. Every couple of minutes I'd nervously poke my head back in. I saw Richard Belzer, Bill Maher, and Richard Lewis hanging out at the bar. These were some of my heroes. I wanted to be a part of their world.

Soon the show was over and everyone piled outside. Budd strolled past me. "Good show tonight," he said. "Call me Monday and I'll give you spots."

He said it in a way that was so quick and matter-of-fact that I wasn't really sure if he'd meant it. The valet arrived with his car and Budd got in. Just before he pulled away, he rolled down his window and said, "Remember to tell me that you're from Philadelphia. That will remind me who you are."

Look, life is full of moments when things don't turn out the way you want them to. But when they do . . .

I called Budd on Monday. "It's Todd Glass," I said, "from Philadelphia?" I got spots at the Improv that week. I got them again the next week, and the week after that.

CHAPTER 23
WORKING THE ROAD

Life in the middle.

A few months after I moved to L.A., Katy and my mom came to visit. My mom wasn't ready to give up on the idea of Katy and me as a couple, which even now I totally understand. We looked like we should have been inseparable. What could possibly stand in the way of us being together?

Katy seemed inclined to believe it was, as my mom said, shyness, and took a more aggressive approach. *I'm sorry*, I was dying to tell her. *I'm not shy, I'm gay!* Instead, I lay through a lot of awkward back massages.

Shortly after they left, I had a new issue to contend with: The Joneses were moving to Connecticut and I had to find a new place to live.

The whole reason I knew Caroline Jones was through

Martha Helfrich, who had been a waitress at Smokey Joe's. Her parents lived in Fountain Valley, about a half hour southwest of Anaheim Hills. Lucky for me, they were getting divorced— ironically because her dad, who was in his midfifties and had fathered eight children, had decided to come out of the closet.

Which is how I wound up living with Mim, Martha's mother, in Fountain Valley. I liked living with Mim—she didn't mind when I had friends over to hang out by her pool, and since she spent a lot of time at another house they had in Maine, I often had the place to myself.

Most of the time, however, I was traveling. Stand-up comedy was exploding all over the country, and if you were willing to put in the miles, there were more places to work than ever before. I still did dates at the L.A. Improv, but mostly I moved among the eleven "road" Improvs that had opened as part of a national expansion.

The club I was most excited about playing was the Las Vegas Improv, then located at the Riviera Hotel & Casino. As a twenty-four-year-old, the only things I knew about Vegas were that you got to see your name on a big sign and to make sure there was plenty of water in your car for the drive through the desert. I pictured a beaten path through the sand and cactuses. I was genuinely shocked when I discovered Vegas and L.A. were connected by a highway. And a little more so when I saw the sign at the Riviera—the free buffet took up a lot more real estate than my name.

But everything else about the club was amazing. I was doing twenty-one shows a week and couldn't have been happier. The maître d' was a guy named Steve Schirripa. Talk about larger than life—Steve personified Vegas to me: a New York guy with a huge personality and sharp suit who knew everyone in town and ran the room like a mafia don. (Years later, Steve got a small part in the Martin Scorsese movie *Casino*, which eventually led to a major role on *The Sopranos* as Tony's brother-in-law Bobby Baccalieri.)

Steve has inspired a lot of legends that may or may not be true. Like the time an older couple from the Midwest gave him a hard time about their seats and he told them to go fuck themselves. Shocked, the husband threatened to file a complaint and demanded Steve's name.

"Steve."

"What's your last name?"

"You tell my boss a guy named Steve told you to go fuck yourself. He'll know who you're talking about."

Or the time a comedian went five minutes longer than he was supposed to. The most important thing to remember when you're working Vegas is to never go over your allotted time—the casinos want their customers gambling as much as possible, and every minute those customers are watching your show is a minute away from the tables. Steve Schirripa sat the comedian down in the back office and pulled out a calculator. "Let's see . . . ," he said. "There were three hundred people at your show. Five minutes of gambling, the casino can expect to make about thirty-five thousand dollars. How much money did your act bring in tonight? I think you owe me about twenty-five thousand dollars. Tell you what . . . I'll let you off the hook this time if you give me the shoes you're wearing. But next time, I tell you to do fifteen minutes, you do fifteen minutes. That's not fifteen minutes and one second, or fourteen minutes and ninety-nine seconds, you with me?"

No, that's not a typo. If Steve said there were ninety-nine seconds in a minute, you were inclined to believe him. I don't know if the stories are true or not, but I'm inclined to believe them based on my own experiences with Steve. One night I was onstage and, no matter what I seemed to do, the audience just wasn't laughing. I decided to do something I'd seen a few other comics do in the past—since the crowd wasn't responding, I turned around to deliver the rest of my act to the brick wall behind me. Until out of nowhere, like the voice of God, Steve Schirripa boomed over the PA: "Todd . . . Turn around and do your fucking act."

He wasn't yelling. He didn't have to. I turned around and did my fucking act. I might have felt a little put out in the moment, but in hindsight, I really respected Steve for that. I like things to be done the right way. And here was a guy in the back of the room who thought, even if this wasn't the best crowd in the world, there was still a right way to do the show. Afterwards, I expected to get a lecture from him, but he never mentioned it again. There was no memo to Budd Friedman. All Steve wanted was for me to turn around and do my fucking act, and once I did, the problem was solved.

Another night—a busy Saturday—I asked Steve if I could get five of my friends in for free. "Are you kidding me?" he said. "On a Saturday? No way. Can't do it." So I was surprised when, after the show, one of my friends thanked me for hooking them up.

"Steve," I said, "did you let my friends in for free?"

"Yeah, I did."

"How did you even know who my friends were?"

"Todd, I saw five preppy people standing in line. Who the fuck else are they friends with?"

When Vegas came to a close, I moved on to the next Improv. Most of the time I was working as the middle, between the opening act and the headliner, making about $850 a week plus lodging. Once in a while, "lodging" meant a nice hotel nearby. More often than that it was a "comedy condo," which was really another way of saying "shitty apartment." Sometimes I'd get the shitty apartment all to myself. Sometimes I'd have to share it with the headliner. The worst was when they crammed all three acts into one place.

But even the worst was pretty good. I remember one Thanksgiving, I found myself sharing a condo in Dallas with then relatively unknown comedians Steve Harvey and John Henton. The two of them took over the shitty apartment's shitty kitchen and cooked a feast, a combination of traditional Thanksgiving dishes and soul food. What impressed me most was the presentation: Here were a couple of guys who I didn't think would care about it at all, but when dinner was served, Steve Harvey said, "Hold up, everybody, we're going to set the table and eat like human beings." We set the table with whatever mismatched utensils we could find and had an amazing dinner.

These days, comedians can't wait to get off the road so they can get back home to focus on their careers. Back then, unless you landed a sitcom, there wasn't anything else to do with your career. I was working—what more could I want? I'd go in on a Wednesday and do shows through Sunday. Sometimes, at the end of my last show, they'd tell me that the act they'd scheduled for the following week had fallen through. "I'll stay!" I'd always yell. If I could have stayed a month at a club, I would have. It was fun.

• • •

I n almost every city I'd hear about a gay bar or neighborhood. I never had the courage to check out either one, but I often wondered what it would be like to live a life where I didn't have to hide, where I'd at least have the option to meet someone without worrying that the whole world was going to find out about me.

Sometimes I'd stay at a club because I had a crush on a guy. It was always a straight guy, because that's all I ever found attractive. And nothing ever happened, because, well, that's what tends to happen when you have crushes on straight guys.

Not that I was entirely celibate. While I would go through long stretches of not doing anything with anyone, once in a while I would meet someone and we'd get drunk enough to overcome our fears and hook up.

But I desperately wanted to meet someone who was more than just a hookup. Someone I could be with around my friends. Someone I really connected with. While I waited for that to happen, I'd take what I could get. And as soon as it was over, I couldn't wait to get out of there and back to my "normal" life.

Sometimes I'd hook up without even trying.

One night after a show at the Tempe Improv, I returned to my condo. I was exhausted and more than a little bit drunk, so when I realized I'd lost my key, instead of panicking, I decided to have a cigarette by the pool and wait for the other comedians to get home. When I finished the cigarette, I lay down on a pool chair and closed my eyes. I was just nodding off when I heard a woman's voice. From the few words we exchanged, I gathered that she had been at my show earlier that night and that she was also very drunk. I fell back on my old strategy to extract myself from the conversation: closing my eyes and pretending to pass out.

She sat down next to me and touched my leg. As drunk, tired, and not interested in a woman blowing me as I was, my dick had other ideas. Suddenly I had a boner and, without missing a beat, the woman unzipped my pants and, well, I couldn't just "wake up" from my imaginary blackout and ask her to stop . . . Well, I probably could have, but I didn't. When it was over she got up and left. I lifted my head off the pool chair to see if anyone saw us. Not that I was scared, just the opposite: I was hoping someone saw us, as that would cement my straight reputation forever. Or at least in Tempe, which probably wouldn't have been the worst place in the world to move.

While no one was around to witness the deed, I did learn something that night: I might be gay, but my dick is definitely bisexual.

CHAPTR 24
TODD GOES TO COLLEGE

Because children are the future.

By the time the '80s came to an end, there was so much demand for stand-up that Budd Friedman opened a second Improv in L.A., or at least Santa Monica, which is where I met Dave Rath.

Dave was the manager at the new club. He and I hit it off right away. Not only was he nurturing toward comedians, but he was a regular guy who didn't act like he was in the business—someone who reminded me of my friends back home.

I was still living with Mim in Fountain Valley, but the commute was getting to be a little much and I was finally ready to move to L.A. I mentioned my plan to Dave, who told me another comedian, Allan Murray, had a house in the Hollywood Hills and was looking for roommates. Dave and I moved in, along with another comedian, Brian Posehn. Brian, I think enough time has passed for me to finally be honest with you: Yes, I was the one who was eating all of your food.

Dave got a job at MTV. The network was just beginning to branch out from music videos into other forms of entertainment, including comedy. They were also notoriously cheap, so Dave volunteered our house as a rent-free option for some of their social events. It's fun to look back at those parties now, where new friends like Adam Sandler, Chris Farley, David Spade, and Rob Schneider could drink and do bits. Sarah Silverman, who was maybe eighteen at the time, sometimes liked to crash on our couch.

My bedroom was in an unfinished part of the house between the garage and a staircase. When I was too lazy to climb two flights of stairs to the nearest bathroom, I stepped outside and peed into the woods. Which is how I met our next-door neighbor, Jay Mohr, who was too lazy to walk down two flights of steps to his bathroom and liked to pee off his deck.

Jay was one of the few people I've met who might love doing bits as much as I do, and we quickly became friends. One night, after a show, we were driving home together down Santa Monica Boulevard. The stretch that passes through West Hollywood is, far and away, L.A.'s most visible gay scene, lined with bars and clubs and happy people spilling out into the street.

"Let's go into a gay bar," Jay said. "It'll be fun."

I should point out here that Jay isn't gay—he's secure enough in his sexuality not to give a shit. As for me, talk about acting: "I don't know . . ." is what I said to Jay, when on the inside I couldn't have been more curious. I'd never set foot in a gay bar before and really wanted to see what it was like.

"Let's have a contest," Jay said, popping a piece of gum into his mouth. "See who gets picked up first."

Within twenty seconds, a guy walked up to Jay and asked, "Do you have any more gum?"

Jay grinned and whispered to me out of the side of his mouth: "I win."

I turned my attention to the club. Everywhere I looked, guys were talking to guys, seemingly confident in who they were and what they wanted. It was all so overwhelming that I looked up at the TV instead. The bar had put together a weird collage of old comedy clips—stand-up routines from *The Tonight Show*; sketches from *Carol Burnett*.

"Todd, we've got to go," Jay said.

"Hold on, hold on . . . Let me just see the end of this bit."

"Todd, if we don't leave right now, I'm going to tell everyone we know that I couldn't get you out of a gay bar."

Jay Mohr's manager, Barry Katz, encouraged me to submit an audition tape to the National Association for Campus Activities. When they selected me, I got to perform at a couple of their showcases, where hundreds of representatives from colleges around the country looked for entertainment that they could bring back to campus. Thanks to Barry, I wound up booking hundreds of college shows.

I loved working colleges. You could feel the energy as you walked around the streets at night. I'd fly in, do shows at three or four schools in the area, then fly out again. Since I still couldn't read a map, I usually looked for students to drive me from one campus to another.

Did I ever feel attracted toward any of them? Sometimes painfully so. But I was always so conscious of not making other people feel uncomfortable that I never pursued it. I kept all of my feelings bottled up. In fact, I did such a good job of hiding my feelings that it occasionally got me into trouble.

One weekend, I met three girls who were part of whatever committee had hired me to come to their school. Not only did they pick me up from the airport, but when I decided to hang around the campus for a couple of days before my next gig, they offered to let me stay at their house.

I told them I had a girlfriend. When I think back to this story now, I realize that those girls must have thought that I had the coolest, most trusting girlfriend on the planet: someone who let me stay in a house with three college girls and never called me once. And why wouldn't she trust me? I was a saint! I was so incredibly faithful, there wasn't even a hint of sexual tension. What a catch!

The National Association for Campus Activities was a little less impressed with my behavior. Word got back to them that one of their comedians had spent the weekend in a house with three college girls. They didn't throw me out of the program, but they did give a stern reprimand.

Which was, in a word, awesome.

I didn't do anything to stop word from spreading; in fact, I did everything in my power to help the story live on for as long as possible. "NACA is really mad at me for spending the weekend with those college girls," I bragged to my friends at lunch a few days later. "But what are you gonna do?"

Cut to the next day, when another comedian asked me if I was still working colleges: "Oh, so you heard about the three hot girls I stayed with at the University of Miami. I'm lucky NACA didn't press charges."

A month later, when my brother asked me how my career was going: "What, did Mom tell you about the three college girls I spent the weekend with? I thought I made her promise not to say anything!"

Three months later, when I got pulled over by a cop: "Pleeeeeease don't tell me this has something to do with those girls I stayed with back in Miami . . ."

The most interesting thing that *actually* happened that weekend was an offhanded comment from one of the girls about a friend of hers who was gay—she spoke about him like it wasn't in any way a big deal. I was only twenty-seven, not much older than these kids, but man, did they seem more progressive and open-minded than some of the people I grew up with.

The world was clearly evolving, a fact that was highlighted to me by a visit from my old high school friend Dave Olsen.

Dave was dating a girl and, like with any serious relationship, he inevitably had to introduce her to his friends. When he did, some of us were surprised to find out that Dave hadn't mentioned the fact that she was black. I know 1991 doesn't seem that long ago, but it was a time when interracial relationships still felt risqué.

Look, let me be perfectly clear here: None of us cared that she was black. That was never the issue. But while some people processed it quickly and quietly, others wondered if maybe a heads-up had been in order. These weren't hateful people—they were evolved enough to know that love was hard enough to find without limiting it to people from any particular race or religion. But couldn't Dave have warned them? "Hey guys, I'm bringing my girlfriend home. Not that it matters, and I know you don't care, but I just wanted to let you know that she's black."

But the more I thought about it, the more I realized that Dave didn't owe anyone a warning, or even an explanation. We have to get to a place as a society where we don't have to mention these things. Dave wasn't waiting for the rest of us to get there; he was out in front, paving the way. This was just one more example of how ahead of his time Dave has always been. He wasn't trying to be a rebel—he just did what he thought was right. Society can't grow and evolve without people like Dave taking the first leap, deciding that they don't have to explain to their friends that their girlfriend is black, or isn't Jewish, or is Jewish, or isn't even a girl.

CHAPTER 25
TWO
NOTEBOOKS

Comedy's gay marriage (between stand-up and sketch).

I couldn't believe what I was feeling, like it was somebody else who'd been doing stand-up for more than ten years. I'd been in front of audiences that were, in some cases, a hundred times as big as this one. But this wasn't the kind of audience I was used to, and they weren't expecting a traditional stand-up performance.

My stomach ached like it did the first time I stepped in front of an open mike. I wasn't even supposed to be performing tonight at the UnCabaret, a club that was helping to push comedy into an interesting new direction—somebody got sick or fell out, and Dave Rath suggested they put me up instead.

"It's good that you have a stomachache," Dave said to me as I paced nervously offstage. "You're stepping outside of your comfort zone."

So I pushed down the butterflies and took the mike. "You know," I began, "I know the point of this scene is to open up. To be real. To tell real stories. So I need to tell you something. I'm going to go deep. I'm going to go real deep. I need to tell you something that I've never told anyone before . . ."

I paused and took a deep breath. Then:

"Dave Rath is gay."

All of which was true, except for the last part about Dave being gay.

It was 1994, and stand-up comedy was beginning to feel stale. Everyone had a theory about what was responsible for the decline, for the news that another club was closing, for the sinking feeling that comedy might be dying.

I knew that comedy wasn't dying. Comedy will never be over. It's like asking if music will be around in thirty years. But anything can get oversaturated. In the beginning, there weren't comedy clubs in every city. Then, all of a sudden, there were. People went, and it was great.

Then there were two clubs in every city. Or three. Pretty soon, some cities had six or seven. The audiences were great, loaded with people who loved stand-up for the same reasons I did. The best comedy movie you'll ever see might deliver twenty or twenty-five big laughs. A great comedian, on the other hand, might make you laugh a hundred times or more during a single forty-five-minute set.

But by 1994, the audiences weren't coming out the way that they used to. Maybe they were getting older or having kids. Maybe they were just noticing what I was noticing: Stand-up comedy was becoming formulaic.

Seinfeld was the number one television show in America;

Home Improvement, starring stand-up comedian Tim Allen, was number two. Paul Reiser's *Mad About You* was also near the top of the ratings. This was the kind of success that every comedian dreamed about. And as far as most comedians were concerned, what worked for Seinfeld would work for them.

The first step was to get on *The Tonight Show*. You needed a "clean seven," seven minutes of great material that could get past the censors on network television. Seinfeld's style of humor quickly became the blueprint that everyone followed.

But Jerry was Jerry—he could dissect everyday things in a way that nobody else could, making observations that would twist back around on themselves at the end. The imitators tended to do a watered-down version of what he did, minus the twists and turns: "Have you ever noticed . . ." was the *setup* to a Jerry Seinfeld bit, a chance to swerve left and right into places that were completely unexpected; for the imitators, the initial observation *was* the entire joke.

The more the formula was repeated, the more audiences started to identify this particular style of comedy with stand-up as a whole. This was frustrating for two reasons: (1) audiences were getting bored of seeing the same style of jokes over and over again; (2) it was the kind of show that audiences had come to expect, and any efforts by comics to diverge from the formula seemed to confuse the crowd, especially at the clubs on the road that "papered" their audiences in order to survive.

The theory behind "papering" was simple: clubs gave tickets away for free, figuring they could make up the money selling food and drink. The good news was, at least in some cases, they were right.

The bad news was that the audiences really started to suck.

Comedy, it seemed to me, had always attracted a special kind of audience—a certain breed that respected what was going on onstage, the way some people respect the opera. And let me tell you, if they started trying to lure people to the opera with free tickets, those audiences would probably blow, too.

Eventually, it was up to the comedians to take matters into their own hands. The idea was simple: It's better to do a unique show for 30 people who really wanted to be there than a formulaic act for 250 randoms dragged in off the street, more focused on nachos and beer than the onstage craft.

It wasn't glamorous, not at the start, anyway. I remember Dave Rath lugging a PA system into any space that would allow him to do comedy—Chinese restaurants, social clubs, an empty lobby, or anywhere else we could set up a makeshift room and put on a show. The upside was absolute creative freedom to do whatever we wanted, as long as it made people laugh.

The UnCabaret, founded in the late '80s by a performance artist named Beth Lapides, was one of the first venues to try something really new. Her show eliminated the idea that an "act" had to be a series of setups and punch lines—the comedians she chose were usually storytellers. Their performances felt unstructured, even stream-of-consciousness.

The format had its naysayers and critics. I heard a lot of people say it was an excuse to do comedy without punch lines. They weren't altogether wrong. There were comedians who, at least in my eyes, used the unstructured format to cover up a lack of preparation. But I didn't look at it from that angle: If I saw a lineup of seven comedians and three or four of them were doing something unique and different, something that didn't feel overprocessed or need a generic "ba-DUMP" at the end of every joke, that felt really exciting to me.

I should say that most of the critics weren't great comics, but rather comedians who had been doing the same road act for years and either saw this new scene as being beneath them or, on a deeper level, were maybe too scared to explore a new direction. Over the years I've seen a lot of great comics like David Spade, Brian Regan, Louis C.K., and Jim Gaffigan play both scenes, moving easily between the mainstream comedy clubs and the random makeshift ones that were popping up all over town.

These new venues attracted a lot of talent from local sketch and improvisational groups. This was where Tenacious D got to perform. Janeane Garofalo. Kathy Griffin. Andy Dick. A mock performance art troupe called Simpatico introduced a lot of local crowds to Will Ferrell. Eventually, Scott Aukerman and B. J. Porter started a show at the M Bar called Comedy Death-Ray that gave this emerging scene a place to thrive.

I loved the way that the stand-up and sketch-comedy scenes seemed to be merging. I remember a bit that began with Scott onstage, doing what seemed like a normal stand-up routine, until Matt Besser started making some noise up in the rafters.

"What's going on up there?" Scott yelled.

"I'm just here to fix the air-conditioning," Matt replied.

"Could you hurry it up? I'm trying to do an act down here."

"Oh . . . I'm sorry. I didn't hear anyone laughing. I thought you were finished." Suddenly, Scott was the shill as Matt proceeded to launch into a devastatingly funny critique of the routine.

And, like I said, the audiences were awesome. They were patient and nurturing and, as a direct reward, reaped the benefits of great comedy. Comedians work best when they're comfortable, producing funny material that in turn leads the audiences to become even more patient and nurturing. While traditional stand-up seemed to be stuck in a rut that was collapsing in on itself, venues like UnCabaret and the M Bar made it feel like comedy was really evolving.

I only got to do UnCabaret once or twice—I wasn't a regular, and I was a little bit jealous of the people who were—but I found a scene of my own at a club called Largo.

As I work through this book, I try to stay really conscious of overdramatizing anything because I don't want to delegitimize the stuff that really happened. But the first time I played Largo was one of those truly dramatic moments. I felt like what I imagine a born-again Christian feels like. I wanted to tell everybody about it. I wanted to bring everybody there.

The crowds were fun and supportive. You could be ironic about stand-up comedy and have the audience get it, or act silly in untraditional ways. It was a place for Dana Gould to get up onstage and tap into something honest and occasionally soulbaring. Or for Paul F. Tompkins, Andy Kindler, Patton Oswalt, David Cross, and Sarah Silverman to look for new ways to make people laugh.

And for me! Adjusting to the new format forced me to do a lot of soul-searching, at least as far as my comedy was concerned. I finally had the opportunity to put into action the advice that Dennis Miller had given me, years earlier, about being myself onstage.

I once did an entire set just mocking the big introductions

that some comedians liked to do, bowing and shaking hands with everyone in the audience and bowing some more for what must have felt like an eternity before walking off without telling a single joke. Another time I spent several minutes trying to remember the details of a bit about my parents' age, eventually getting so flustered that I had to pull out my phone and pretend to call my mom.

When you talk about being "real" onstage, a lot of people think that means expressing strong political views or digging into some kind of social realism. Yes, those are ways of being real, but real can also be a silliness you tap into. Steve Martin is a brilliant comedian who has never said a word about social issues or done anything political—his brilliance comes out of his unique style of silliness. I didn't want to be Steve Martin, but I wanted to do what he did, tapping into the silliness that I felt in my gut. This new scene gave me the chance to try. I started keeping two notebooks: one for the traditional material I used mainly on the road; one for the experimental material I could whip out at places like Largo.

CHAPTER 26
FINALLY

Todd meets somebody.

As a comedian, I felt more invigorated than I had in years. As for the rest of my life, well, it left me wanting more.

Or anything. I wanted to have a relationship that went deeper than just fooling around. But I was still running into the same old problem: Every guy I was attracted to turned out to be straight.

I didn't know how to meet people who were like me. Gay bars clearly weren't my scene. Sometimes, maybe once every year or two, I'd stumble into a random hookup. But most of my love life involved hoping for opportunities that never materialized.

Goddamn was I frustrated. Sometimes doing stand-up for a living felt like a curse—it was a fun thing for guys to do, so *of course* they'd come when you'd invite them to a show. *Of course* I was going to think that they really liked me. Most of them wouldn't even look at girls when they went out with me. What took me a while to realize is that I was confusing their interest in me as a comedian with some deeper level of attraction. Tonight they were hanging out with a stand-up comic; they could get laid any other night of the week.

I was always so careful. I said nothing, revealed nothing, and did everything in my power to keep sex out of the conversation. I liked to imagine that someday I'd find the courage to open up to the world, which would be terrifying enough without people going, "Oh! So *that's* why he made me so uncomfortable that night." I didn't want any stories out there. No matter how powerful the crush, I never did anything.

I felt one of those crushes coming on one night after I did a show at the Comedy & Magic Club in Hermosa Beach. He was a waiter there, just hanging out in the greenroom after the show chatting with some of the other comics. I knew that he was straight. But for some reason, when I started talking to him, I mentioned that I was headed to a Halloween party later at a friend's house and that he should come. Which I quickly followed, in my typically self-conscious way, by inviting everyone in the room to come, too.

I didn't think there was any way he was going to go. But as everyone began to leave, he asked me for the address. A little while later, we were at the party, the two of us sitting on the kitchen counter, just talking and talking and drinking and talking and drinking some more. His sense of humor and way of looking at the world reminded me of onetime best friend Katy, only this time, Katy was a guy.

The more I drank, the more I started to feel like a fifteen-year-old. I started saying the kinds of things that a drunk, awkward, fumbling fifteen-year-old might say:

"There's something I want to tell you—there's someone at this party that I really, really like."

"Who?" replied the waiter, who I'd since learned had a name: Chris.

"I don't want to tell you."

"Why?"

"It might make them feel uncomfortable."

"Why would it make them uncomfortable?"

"I don't know."

"Tell me."

"What if it was you?"

Chris paused and looked down at his drink. "Ah, dude . . . that's not me. I'm not into that."

Fuckfuckfuck! Not only did I feel like shit, but I was petrified. Tomorrow he'd go back to his job at the club and tell everyone that I hit on him. "I'm going outside to smoke a cigarette," I said.

I was a little bit surprised when Chris came outside to join me. We walked around the block. Then we turned a corner and he surprised me again: He pulled me in close and kissed me.

We both ended up crashing at my friend's house that night—me on the couch and Chris on the floor, both of us terrified that someone would suspect that something had happened. By the time I woke up the next morning, he was gone. I got into my car. A few blocks from the house, I pulled over and started to cry.

I was so fucking tired. The way I was leading my life was taking an enormous emotional toll on me. Even though Chris and I had exchanged numbers, I knew we'd never use them. Plenty of people have one-night stands and never see one another again—sometimes you know right away that you're not going to be compatible. But this situation didn't have anything to do with incompatibility; in fact, it felt like the opposite was true. Everything had been easy. We'd talked for hours while the party seemed to disappear around us. This should have been the start of something—a first date. But I was hiding who I was, and he was twenty-two and confused about what he was feeling. The only future we had was the discomfort we'd both feel the next time I returned to the Comedy & Magic Club. It would probably be best for both of us if I avoided the club altogether.

I don't know how long I sat there before I drove home, deciding to put last night, Chris, and everything else away for now.

We didn't have cell phones yet. The light on my answering machine was blinking when I walked into my room. It was Chris, asking if I wanted to go see a show with him that night. I called him back immediately and left a message on his machine. In his return message he left three of his numbers—"Here's my home, my work, and my pager."

Holy shit. He really wants me to call him back!

CHAPTER 27
TODD'S COMA

New relationship, new friends, and new professional opportunities.

Chris and I went out again that night. And the next night after that. We seemed to connect on every level, laughing at the same jokes and sharing a similar appreciation for doing absolutely nothing. Before we knew it, we were in a new relationship, which felt amazing—except for the part where I couldn't share it with anyone.

My friend Chris. That's how I introduced him to people when he came to pick me up on the set of *Married . . . with Children*, where I was filming a guest spot. I told everyone that my friend Chris and I were going out to lunch at a nearby restaurant.

"Hey, I was going to drop my car off near there," said Ed O'Neill, the star of the show. "You think you could give me a ride back?"

We parked illegally in an alley and met Ed at the dealership. By the time the three of us got back to my car, it was being wheeled onto a flatbed tow truck.

I did my best to reason with the tow truck driver. When that didn't work, I got down on my knees and begged. The guy wouldn't have it.

"I know what to do," Chris whispered in my ear. "Just walk around the corner to the other side of the building." Ed looked at me quizzically. I shrugged—I didn't have a clue. We walked around the corner as Chris approached the tow truck driver, asking if he could retrieve his medicine from the back of the car.

Ten seconds later, I heard the motor rev and the tires screech as Chris backed the car off the truck, hitting the ground with a thud. Ed and I started walking a little faster, looking to put some distance between us and the tow truck driver, who was unleashing a string of expletives at the car, which was already disappearing around the corner.

Ed and I made it to the other side of the building. It was hard to tell what part of the experience felt stranger—that I was on the run with TV's Al Bundy, or that I was in a new relationship with a guy who was capable of doing something this crazy. Chris pulled over and picked us up. The three of us cracked up all the way back to the set.

"I loved the way your friend handled that," Ed said the next day. I was starting to love the way "my friend" did a lot of things, a feeling that I wanted to share with Ed and the rest of the world. But I still wasn't ready to tell anyone about my *situation*. Chris and I were both determined to keep our relationship a secret, adding a difficult and occasionally comedic element to our lives.

I'd recently moved into a new house with another comedian, Mike Koman. Mike was only nineteen but looked ten years
older. Young comedians are fun to hang out with because they
tend to be obsessed with comedy in the same way that I still
am—even though I've been at it for thirty years, I can still talk
comedy thirty hours a day. (And I still suck at math.) Mike and
I hit it off immediately. He was looking for a place to live with
James Milton, a friend of his from school. The three of us wound
up renting a huge house up in the Hollywood Hills.

My room had its own entrance, so most nights Chris would
sneak in. On one of those nights, Mike knocked on the door
to my room and let himself in before I could stop him. Chris
moved like a maniac, flopping out of the bed and onto the
floor, where Mike literally had to step over him to walk in. *Mike
has to fucking know, right? I mean, what could he have possibly
thought? Just two normal straight guys hanging out in my room, one
in the bed, the other on the floor in his boxers. Totally normal!*

Mike and James were only about ten years younger than
me, but it was pretty clear that they came from a different gen-
eration. They talked about their gay friends in a very matter-
of-fact way: "Joe's boyfriend is in town on Monday, so we're all
going to go out then." They never snickered, added editorial
comments, or even raised an eyebrow; they might as well have
been talking about a straight couple. It wasn't just that they
were okay with someone being gay—sexuality, to them, was
an unimportant detail, like having brown hair. It didn't seem to
confuse them the way that it did me.

I had a tooth pulled and the dentist prescribed Vicodin. I
had never taken Vicodin before and was feeling great. It dawned

on me that if I couldn't tell these two guys in my chemically re-laxed state, I'd never be able to tell anybody.

I sat Mike and James down on the couch. Despite (or maybe because of) the Vicodin, I hemmed and hawed and took maybe fifteen minutes to spit it out. "You had to know, right?" I finally asked.

"Nope," Mike said.

While I'd never come out to any of my friends before, I'd talked to other gay people about what the experience had been like for them. The best situations seemed to involve parents or friends who were not only supportive in the moment, but fol-lowed up later with acceptance. The worst involved horror and rejection. But most of these stories tended to fall into a middle ground: support and acceptance in the moment of the confes-sion, then never mentioned again. This always seemed sad and weird to me, like people were saying, "I know we're supposed to be okay with this, and we are, *for the most part*, but maybe we shouldn't mention it again for a while . . ."

If it really wasn't a big deal, people would be curious, bom-barding you with questions. *What's it like? When did you know? Do you have a boyfriend?* But here I was with Mike and James, who weren't asking me anything at all. *I knew it! They're uncomfortable. Great job, Todd!*

Or so I thought. A few days later, we were going out to dinner and James casually asked me if Chris was coming. The lightbulb went on in my head: *They weren't asking me questions because there wasn't anything that they really needed to know.* It reminded me of Dave Olsen and the nonissue of his fiancée. You hear people talk all the time about what's wrong with kids today, but here was a moment when I realized how incredibly cool youth could be. They really, honestly, truly did not give a fuck, and that made me feel good.

Being around Mike and James was great for other reasons, too. One day I came home from an audition feeling miserable. I hated going on auditions. I still do—the audition process just doesn't work for me, for reasons that I'll get into a couple of chapters from now. "I'm done with auditions," I joked to Mike. "I just want to be on a show where I'm in a coma, so I don't have to do anything but lay there."

"That's not a bad idea," Mike replied.

We were still talking about it at three in the morning. Most shows center around some kind of meeting place that brings all the characters together—why couldn't it be a guy in a coma? His family could visit. Friends would tell stories about how they met him. We'd make up anything we wanted about his life pre-coma and just tell it through the eyes of the people coming to visit him. Mick Jagger could show up and say, "Bloody shame—he used to be a roadie for the band."

We decided to shoot our own pilot. By now, video cameras had become a lot more affordable and, with the right computer software, you could edit the material yourself. We'd recently added a fourth roommate, Steve Rosenthal, who brought a diligent professionalism to the project we'd started referring to as *Todd's Coma*. We reached out to the people we wanted to help us make it. I asked Sarah Silverman. Steve emailed the famous jazz musician Herb Alpert, who had just done a Gap commercial—we convinced Herb to play a nurse who denies that he used to be Herb Alpert. Another friend of mine played softball with Fred Willard, whom I'd been obsessed with since watching *Fernwood 2Night* with my dad. And Chris, well . . .

We were at a party together when we saw Ben Stiller. I'd been introduced to Ben years earlier by Judd Apatow—the three of us wound up doing Don Rickles impressions all night—and I thought that Ben might remember me. "Go talk to him," Chris said. "See if he'll do *Todd's Coma*."

"I'm too embarrassed," I confessed.

"Hey, Todd," I heard Chris saying a minute later. "You know Ben, right?"

Oh Jesus.

"Tell him about your idea!" Chris added.

I wanted to punch Chris in the face. I felt like a little kid being pushed by his proud parents to recite a poem for their friends. But the pitch wasn't complicated so I just started talking, pausing every two minutes to give Ben an out.

Ben could see that I was uncomfortable. "Do I look like you're bothering me?" he said every time I paused. "I'm going away in two days, but FedEx me a few of the ideas you want me to do."

Two months later, I was lying on a mattress in the middle of my living room while Ben Stiller, Fred Willard, Sarah Silverman, Jimmy Pardo, and Herb Alpert rehearsed around me. It was surreal, to say the least.

We pitched the show to a bunch of production companies, but nothing happened until, about six months later, the comedian Nick Swardson noticed our video gathering dust on a shelf in Adam Sandler's office. Nick encouraged Adam to watch the show. With Adam's help, we sold the pilot to TBS.

Almost overnight, I had offices on the Sony lot and a million-dollar budget. I was pulling in every day through the gate, just like I'd seen in the movies. I got to hire Steve Rosenthal and Mike Koman—Adam's theory was if these were the two guys who helped you create it, why wouldn't you want them on board? We met with production designers and wardrobe stylists.

I remember driving to the shoot on the first day, getting off the 405 and seeing big signs with arrows that said *Todd's Coma*. There were caterers and cameramen, police officers on motorcycles blocking traffic so we could shoot a scene in the middle of the street.

All because I was bad at acting and didn't want to audition anymore.

The show never got picked up. (You can still find it on YouTube, if you're interested.) While I obviously wished it had been a huge success, I still look back on the experience—no bullshit—as one of the most amazing opportunities I've ever had. (Thank you, Adam Sandler!) I didn't have anything to get bitter about: My new relationship, new roommates, and new professional opportunities had me overflowing with confidence. For the first time I was beginning to feel normal and secure in my whole life, not just the part that I was showing to the world.

CHAPTER 28
TODD'S SITUATION

Thank God for Andrea.

It didn't take long for my relationship with Chris to escalate. We were spending nearly all of our free time together.

I was getting ready to go to Dallas for a gig when he surprised me with a suggestion.

"What if I came with you?"

As much as I wanted him to, I was also terrified. What would I say to the other comedians? None of them had ever seen me with a female companion; in fact, I'd go out of my way to ignore any woman who approached me after a show. Now there was a guy staying in my room with me? They'd have to know, right? I held off saying yes for as long as I could, but in the end, my desire to spend more time with Chris and to share this part of my life with him won out over my fears.

We had a great time. Even better, no one seemed to be the wiser about our relationship. Feeling more confident, I started bringing Chris with me to other clubs.

We had to tell people something, so we said that he was my brother. To be honest, we probably didn't spend as much time as we should have thinking through our cover story. When Chris's dad—who is Chinese—came to our house to visit, we found ourselves scrambling to come up with a coherent story to tell our friends. After that, Chris became my stepbrother.

When people talk about hiding "in the closet," I don't think they really know what that means. I like to say it means everything you're *not* thinking. It's like keeping plates spinning in the air, all day, every day. Staying closeted isn't a black-and-white issue—it's full of nuances and moving parts. We had to keep track of who knew about us. Who didn't. Who did but wasn't saying anything. We felt like undercover cops trying to remember which cover stories we'd shared with what people. In retrospect, with all the lies and the stories and the hours and hours we spent trying to stay in character, it's pretty amazing that I don't have a better acting career.

Which is why we were so lucky to have Andrea.

I met Andrea after one of my shows. Besides being tall, stunningly beautiful, and smart, she was hilarious. Chris told her about us very early on—Chris was usually more comfortable telling women about our situation, while I was generally most comfortable telling, well, nobody. But all three of us felt comfortable spending lots of time together. In fact, the three of us became so tight that we decided to buy a house together. Andrea was a teacher and secured a low-interest loan through her credit union; Chris and I scraped together the down payment.

People knew we were looking for a new place to live. "Have you and Chris found a house yet?" they'd ask.

"You mean me and Chris and *Andrea*," I'd instantly correct them. "Yes, me and Chris and Andrea are still looking for a house." Andrea. AndreaAndreaAndreaAndrea. I'd say her name so many times that it would spin people around, getting them so dizzy they'd stop asking me questions.

But panic set in whenever Chris and I were spotted running errands together. Especially if those errands were at a place like Bed Bath & Beyond. One day we were there buying stuff for the house, when a comedian friend of mine walked over to say hello. "Todd! What are you doing here?"

I looked at Chris, who was maybe five feet away from me. *Oh shit! We can't be seen at Bed Bath & Beyond together. It looks so . . . gay!*

Chris didn't have to read my mind—we'd already worked out a protocol for situations just like this one: He quickly walked away without turning back. "Oh, just looking for some stuff," I replied. "I just bought a house with my friend Andrea and she wanted me to buy some things and AndreaAndreaAndreaAndrea . . ."

Our new home was a duplex—Chris and I took the ground floor, while Andrea took the upstairs—and we set about creating our own little world. Andrea was always down to play someone's girlfriend. She got a dinner, drinks, a free night on the town, and, at the end of the evening, no one tried to fuck her. It didn't always work though—after all, Andrea was a beautiful woman and once in a while she forgot what her role was. Like when Chris took her to a wedding and she wound up getting drunk and making out with some random guy: "We're not exactly dating," Chris had to explain nervously to the confused people at his table. "We're more like friends with benefits." After that we kept Andrea to a three-drink maximum, checking in with her periodically to make sure she was still in character.

But Andrea was always a good sport. One time we were renting a cabin with a group of our friends. We stopped on the way to load up on groceries for a big dinner we were planning. Chris wanted to get flowers for the table, but was embarrassed at how that might make him look to the others, so he casually tossed them in Andrea's basket.

"Who bought the flowers?" one of our friends inevitably asked when we got to the counter.

Thank God for Andrea. "I did!" she said, just like we asked her to.

But Chris overcompensated. "I can't believe you bought fucking flowers," he said dismissively.

Andrea's eyes looked like they were going to burn a hole right through him. It was absurd what we put her through. When we had dinner parties and wanted to set a fancy table, we would sit Andrea down beforehand and prepare her like she was about to start an undercover sting operation.

"What are you going to say if someone asks who set the table?"

"I'm going to say that I did it."

"Good. And you're going to say it just that way, right? Not like the other time, when someone asked and you said, 'Oh, I did it, but it was no big deal—it only took me a minute.'"

"No, Todd, I'll say it the way you want me to say it."

Sure enough, someone complimented the setting at our dinner party, and Andrea gamely jumped in and took the credit.

We hadn't planned on one of Andrea's friends deciding to correct her. "Andrea didn't set it," she blurted out. "Todd did! He just didn't want anybody to know."

I froze. Chris jumped in and quickly changed the topic: "Why don't you tell everyone about the guy you fucked in the Jacuzzi in Florida?" he asked her.

I was still angry even after most of the guests had gone. "Why did she have to open her big mouth?" I complained to my friend Jimmy Dore, who had stuck around to help us clean up.

Jimmy just laughed. "Don't you hear what you're saying, Todd? You don't want anyone to know that you like pretty things!"

We didn't know how good we had it with Andrea until we got into situations where she wasn't around. When you live in Los Angeles, it's not uncommon for police helicopters to buzz past your house in the middle of the night, shining spotlights that always seem to be directed toward your yard. One night, in the midst of another routine helicopter manhunt, the police knocked on our door and wanted to know if they could continue the search in back of our house.

Obviously we were terrified—not because of the possibility that a dangerous fugitive was hiding in our backyard, but because the policemen might look around our house and get the impression that we were gay. Chris ran to "my" bedroom—the room that had become our storage closet—and started pulling all of the boxes and suitcases off the bed so that it could conceivably look slept in.

"Put those flowers away, they look gay!" Chris screamed.

"You know what looks gay?!" I screamed back at him. "Two men our age living together!"

Throughout it all, we laughed a lot. My personal life was finally catching up with my professional success. But keeping my personal life a secret all of the time not only felt wrong, but was proving harder and harder to do. I'd find myself wanting to share stories about the funny things that happened to Chris and me, so I tried changing certain details to make them fit our cover story.

Like the time Chris and I threw a party at the house and his mother, Pierrette, accidentally ate five pot cookies someone brought with them. My friend Gina, who had been chatting with Pierrette for a few minutes, came into the kitchen to ask me if everything was okay.

"What do you mean?"

"Well, Chris's mom asked me if it was normal to do this . . ." Gina proceeded to wave her hands in front of her face, staring at her fingers as she wiggled them.

"Oh my God!" I yelled, realizing what had happened. "What did you tell her?"

"That it was fine?"

Five pot cookies would have put Willie Nelson on the floor. As the cookies kicked in, Chris's mom—who is French and speaks with a heavy accent—started to moan. We started to panic. Someone called 911. When we told them that pot cookies were involved, they sent an ambulance *and* a police car.

A few minutes later there was a huge scene playing out in front of our house. I should tell you that Pierrette is fine now—in fact, she was fine later that night, flirting heavily with a paramedic forty years her junior as they wheeled her into the ambulance. When she woke the next morning, Pierrette had already decided that the incident was amusing enough to share with all of our neighbors. Needless to say, none of this was particularly amusing to Chris.

"Mom, they're gonna think you're some drugged-up whore!"

A few months later, I decided to tell the story to a group of comedians. For some reason I got worried that using Pierrette as a character might reveal too much about our, *ahem*, situation, so I pretended the story was about my own mother. Halfway through, I realized that I'd unintentionally given my mother a French accent.

So did Dave Rath. "Wait, Todd . . . Why is your mom French in this story?"

I started to sweat. *This is it . . . They're gonna find out . . . How am I going to get out of this one?* Luckily, Sarah Silverman—who by this time had become one of my closest friends and knew all about Chris—jumped in to rescue me. "Oh, that's just Todd being silly," she said.

It worked—this time. But the moment of panic reminded me how exhausting it was to keep living two separate lives. Something had to give.

CHAPTER 29
FIRST RELATIONSHIP

Where Todd learns that men are from Mars, but also from Venus.

By the time most people reach their early thirties, they've spent enough time in relationships to have picked up at least a few of the tools they need to get along with their romantic partners. Not me—I was starting from scratch. Despite our ten-year age difference, Chris and I were entering our relationship from a pretty similar place in terms of emotional maturity.

That place being "little to none." There were bound to be a few speed bumps.

Like the way I'd always been attracted to straight-seeming guys. I'd always had issues with gay men who were more experienced than I was, probably out of jealousy that they were comfortable with their sexuality in a way that I wasn't. With Chris,

I found myself in the strange and unfamiliar position of being the (slightly) more experienced guy.

Eew, gross.

I didn't want to weird Chris out in the way I had been weirded out in the past, so I tried to avoid any conversation about my previous partners. But the topic inevitably came up from time to time and always caused a fight.

There were plenty of arguments over much simpler things. What car I was going to buy. How many weeks I'd be on the road. Which cities were okay for Chris to come visit me in, and which ones weren't. Every couple fights, of course, but neither of us knew how to have a productive conversation that could lead to a mature resolution. There was a lot of screaming. Many doors were slammed in anger.

We finally decided to get professional help. We heard that a local Gay & Lesbian Center offered relationship counseling to same-sex couples. True to form, we parked several blocks away from the therapist's office, near a YMCA, so if Chris and I ran into anyone that we knew we could tell them that we were on our way to the gym. (Because that wouldn't sound gay at all.)

The therapist encouraged us to take time-outs. Everyone thinks time-outs are for kids, but I get it now. They work. (And if they don't, you've got a pretty clear indication that you need more intense help.) I had my doubts at the beginning—*Okay, I'll take a time-out, but two hours from now I'm still going to be mad*—but was amazed to discover that just three minutes in another room and suddenly I was receptive to hearing whatever it was that Chris was really saying to me.

The listening part turned out to be really important. I discovered that I'd been taking a lot of things that Chris said personally, as opposed to being able to listen to him and to figure out where he was coming from. Sometimes the person you're with just wants to be heard. They're not necessarily upset with you—they're just upset and you happened to be there.

We found out that almost every argument has an "over-reactor" and a "calmer-downer"—one person tends to get upset, leading his or her partner to try and defuse the situation by pointing out that whatever it is isn't worth getting upset about. Unfortunately this can sometimes make the overreactor feel like the calmer-downer is trivializing the issue.

So I came up with a way to defuse this dynamic: If the person you're with is upset about something, you just get more upset about it. In other words, the calmer-downer becomes the overreactor, forcing the overreactor to calm down.

"Can you believe we ordered forty-five minutes ago and our food still isn't here?"

"WHAT?! THIS IS TOTAL BULLSHIT! WE ARE SO FUCKING OUT OF HERE!"

"All right, all right. Calm down. It's not a big deal."

"Oh, it's not? Okay, whatever you say."

Or:

"Hey, did you remember to take the laundry from the washer and put it into the dryer?"

"FUCK! I TOTALLY FORGOT! I'M A WORTHLESS PIECE OF SHIT AND DON'T DESERVE YOU! I'M GOING TO GO KILL MYSELF NOW BECAUSE I'M SUCH A FUCKING LOSER!"

"Jesus, relax! I'll do it."

We slowly began to deal with our relationship issues in a way that started to resemble maturity. Our progress even gave me enough courage to bring Chris back to Philadelphia with me where—because it was starting to get a little ridiculous—I finally opened up to my mother and her new husband. It may have taken me thirty-two years, but I'm happy to say that the experience turned out to be a positive one: Nobody said or did anything dramatic. After a lot of routine questions about our relationship ("How long have you been together? Where did you meet?"), Chris was welcomed into our family. I even managed to tell Katy, finally bringing our relationship to an honest place.

But to 99 percent of the other people we ran into, I introduced Chris as my "friend." There was no way I was ready to add those three letters to the front of the word. I really don't know who I was fooling, or even if I was fooling anyone at all, but for now, this was the way it was going to be.

The bigger problem arose when I was onstage. Relationships are full of funny moments and hilarious insights—in other words, great material. I just needed to find a way to talk about my relationship without really talking about my relationship.

At first, I tried to disguise it, setting up jokes with lines like, "You know what I've noticed with my brother and his wife?" After a while, I felt confident enough to start using "my girlfriend" as part of my act.

"So," I've had people ask me, "you had to make up all of those stories?" No! I may have taken liberties with gender, but I didn't make anything up. Every joke I told about my imaginary girlfriend was based on something that had actually happened between Chris and me. It's an experience that taught me something—two things, actually:

First of all, the issues that arise between same-sex couples are almost exactly the same as the ones that come up between heterosexual couples. Granted, there may have been a few restrictions: A bit that started with, "So I'm peeing next to my girlfriend in the bathroom at the airport . . . ," probably would have confused most audiences. But the stories I told always got laughs from what I assume were mostly straight audiences because, at the end of the day, the experiences aren't very different.

Which gets to the second thing I learned: We're all dealing with the same problems. Over the years, I've spent hours listening to men complain about their girlfriends ("You know what's wrong with women?") and women complain about their boyfriends ("What is up with guys?"). Well, guess what? There wasn't a woman in my relationship, but I had a lot of the same issues that my guy friends had with their girlfriends . . . and a lot of the same issues the girls have had with their boyfriends.

The bottom line is this: There are fucked-up men. There are fucked-up women. Sometimes you end up dating or even marrying them. But in the end, the issues are the issues, and we're all trying to work them out. We all have baggage. The trick is making sure that it's carry-on, so we don't turn our partners into bellhops.

CHAPTER 30
LAST COMIC STANDING

Did you get my fax?

Most comedians move to Los Angeles because they want to further their career. It's usually not until they get there that they realize what furthering their career really means: auditions.

As I mentioned earlier, auditions have always been very hard for me. There are plenty of reasons why, but most of them stem from my days in school. I still have a hard time reading. I have an even harder time reading when I'm supposed to be concentrating on something else at the same time, like staying in character or hitting my marks—I can't have two things going on in my head at once. I can barely keep track of one. The second I feel the pressure, I get nervous and sweat pours out of my body.

A couple of years ago I did an episode of *Louie*. It was a

simple scene—all I had to do was walk down the aisle of an airplane, talking on a cell phone. I'd spent the night before memorizing my lines (or, more accurately, my *line*) and felt like I was good to go. But as I was about to start, Louis said, "When you pull out the phone, can you cheat a little bit to the right?"

"Okay, cheat to the right."

"And when you stop to talk to the other passenger, I know you're stopping where most people stop, because that's what you'd do if you were really talking, but I want you to stop around four feet away."

Are you shitting me? I can't remember all that and still deliver my lines. Who the fuck could? (Answer: most actors. They do it all the time. It's actually not that hard if you don't have ADD and dyslexia.)

Later on, I confessed my struggles to Louis. "It's funny you say that," he said. "You remember the first time you auditioned for my show?" He was talking about his first TV show, *Lucky Louie*. HBO was looking for somebody to play Louis's costar, and someone suggested me.

When I get to an audition, the first thing I try to do is figure out a way to read my part sitting down—that way I don't have to worry about hitting marks and I can sneak a quick glance at the script on my lap if I run into trouble. It doesn't really matter what the audition is:

"Okay, you're a cop, and you're chasing the robbers on foot . . ."

"Great! You mind if I sit down for this?"

"In this scene you're jogging with your friend and talking about your date last night . . ."

"Got it. Let me just take a seat over here."

"You're a waiter who keeps coming back to the table . . ."

"Wouldn't it be funnier if I was sitting at the table with the customers?"

I managed to stay seated through the whole audition for *Lucky Louie*. The minute I left the room, Louis looked at the producers. "Are you all thinking what I'm thinking?"

"He's the fucking guy!" they said.

"Yeah, he's the fucking guy!" Louis said.

Chris Albrecht, who knew comedy from his time managing the New York Improv, was running HBO. Like it or not, I've got to give him credit: He sensed there was something a little bit odd about my performance. "Let's get him back in here for a minute," he said.

Someone called me back into the room. "We'd like to try the scene again," the casting director said apologetically. "Only this time, can you walk around the room while you do it?"

"You got me!" is what I should have said. Instead, I did the audition again, this time on my feet. Needless to say, I wasn't the fucking guy, and Louis found another costar.

Commercial auditions were even worse. They made me feel like I was back on a yellow bus driving to school. They made me sick the night before; they made me sick the day of; they made me sick the day after, thinking how bad I did the day before. (I'm starting to feel a little sick right now just writing about auditions.) My manager at the time, Bruce Smith, was pretty good about booking commercials for his clients, so I was nauseous about five days a week. The worst moments were the evenings when seven o'clock would roll around and I didn't have any auditions the next day—*Yes!*—only to have Bruce call me: "Hey, guess what? Good news! I got you a reading for Kia tomorrow . . ."

Cue the stomachache.

Most of the people who were casting commercials were great—the majority of the time they went out of their way to be friendly and accommodating. That didn't help. I would totally blow the reading, and someone would say, "Why don't you go out into the hall, come back in, and you'll do it again?" Or, "Do you want to come back in on Monday?"

NOOOOOOO!!! Let me go! Please let me just go home now.

"Let's do it again, only this time we want you to try . . ."

Okay, I'll do it again, but are you okay that I'm going to do it exactly the same way?

I know that auditions are a necessary part of the process— I'm not blaming anybody but myself for the constant stomach pain—but I think I hate them for the same reasons I love stand-up comedy. When you're performing onstage, you are the writer, the producer, the director, the editor, and the star. If the joke bombs, you can't blame anyone else. (Well, there's always the crowd . . . the sound system . . . the lights . . . the comic who came up before you . . . but other than that it's you.)

Auditions feel like the opposite, especially commercial auditions, which are based primarily on the way you look. They tend to cast two kinds of people: the drop-dead gorgeous, and their best friend, who maybe isn't ugly, but isn't that great-looking, either. The first time I walked into an audition and saw a roomful of drop-dead gorgeous people, I smiled. *So this is what I look like!* Then some guy with a clipboard glanced at me and said, "You must be here for Clearasil. That's down the hall." By the time I got to the end of the hallway, I had a much more accurate idea of how I really looked.

Sometimes it's so arbitrary your looks don't matter. One time I decided *not* to go on an audition. I just didn't feel like going, so I blew it off. The next day, my manager called. "Good news, Todd . . . You got a callback from Chevrolet."

He's fucking with me, I thought. *He knows I blew it off and now he's fucking with me.* I decided to call his bluff: "Oh good! When is it?"

"Tomorrow morning."

"Oh. Good. Great. I mean, I thought I did a good job. Okay, well, you know, fax me over the information."

"I will."

"I'm sure you will. Thanks for the call."

Turns out, he wasn't fucking with me. I'd really earned a callback for an audition I didn't even go on. And yes, I ended up landing the part.

But I still hated the whole process. I remember finding out that my friend Andy Kindler didn't bother with commercials. "Do we really have to go on auditions?" I moaned to my manager like a whiny teenager. "Why do I have to if Andy doesn't?"

"Todd, you're a full-grown adult. You don't have to do anything you don't want to do."

His words were on my mind when I went for what would turn out to be my last commercial audition. Like I said, most of the people involved in the casting process are actually very nice. But then there are the other people: the ones who are bitter about having to videotape two hundred people at a cattle call so that the client can look at thirty. "Okay, everybody come over here," said the casting director, like he was talking to a group of unruly second-graders. "No one is doing this right. The guy in the ad isn't *happy*, he's *excited*. And he's not *disappointed*; it's more like he's *bummed out*. Not *anxious*, but *frustrated*. Has everyone got that?"

Now I didn't know what the fuck this guy was talking about, but he seemed pretty confident about what he wanted. "Hey!" I said. "You sound like you know what to do. Maybe you should do it!" The line got a couple of snickers, just not from the casting director. I walked out of the audition, clearly having impressed no one.

Well, maybe not *no one*. A few years later, I was at the Improv and Nick Swardson was telling me about a hilarious comedian that I had never seen before. So I walked down the hall to catch Zach Galifianakis doing a set and, within two minutes, I fucking loved this guy. After the show, Nick introduced me to Zach.

"Actually, we've met once before," Zach said. He'd been on that same audition and had seen me storm out. He was so amused by the pathos of it all that he'd stolen my Polaroid from the casting director and had held on to it ever since.

While I knew I hated commercial auditions, I was more conflicted when I heard about the tryouts for the second season of a TV show called *Last Comic Standing*. It was a reality show that put ten aspiring comics in a house somewhere in the Hollywood Hills, wired with microphones and about sixty or seventy cameras, and let them compete against one another until there was a winner. The show was hosted by my old neighbor and fellow outdoor peeing enthusiast Jay Mohr.

I didn't know if I wanted to do it. Reality shows weren't

really my thing and I suspected that they were more likely to damage my career than do me any long-term good. But I'd seen what Last Comic Standing had done for the Season One contestants—you couldn't argue with the fact that being on the show had helped their careers.

I was still on the fence the night before the tryouts. I probably wouldn't have gone if it hadn't been for Scott Aukerman and B. J. Porter, the guys who did Comedy Death-Ray. "This is a chance to do your act on network TV in front of millions of people," they reminded me. "You really think you're past that point in your career?"

Lucky for me, the audition process just meant doing my routine in front of a few judges at the Improv. They flew me to New York for a second audition. Then a third in Las Vegas.

I'll admit it: By the time I got through the third audition, I really wanted it. When they called my name, I remember doing a Fuck yeah!

Then I had to do the show.

It should have been easy for me. A reality show. All I had to do was be myself, which might have been fine—if I wasn't hiding a part of who I was. I could bring a noisy fan with me to help cover up my snoring, but concealing my sexuality in a house where every word and action was being filmed and recorded? I might as well have had to memorize a script.

When you're on a reality show, you really do forget that there are people watching your every move. You might glance into the refrigerator one day and wonder out loud to another comedian why there isn't any orange juice. The next day, the fridge will be stocked with four different brands—an odd coincidence, until you remember that you're wearing a microphone.

One night I snuck downstairs for a midnight snack and accidently dropped a glass bottle, which shattered all over the floor. Before I could finish shouting whatever expletive popped into my head, a door sprung open. A guy I'd never seen before emerged with a broom and swept it all up.

Okay, having secret elves to clean up after me was pretty cool. But the phone calls to the outside world were another story. They let me switch my microphone off when I called Chris, but I knew that I was still surrounded by cameras and probably more microphones.

Fortunately, Chris and I were already used to hiding. We worked out a series of codes beforehand so that we could communicate with one another. "Did you get my fax?" meant "I love you." "Can you resend that email?" meant "I miss you." As an added benefit, keeping our relationship secret made my career seem a lot more thriving than it was—I was clearly waiting on a lot of faxes and emails.

My biggest fear was that one of the other comedians would out me. I went into the house with the naïve idea we were going to spend nights around the fire talking comedy. "Who's better, Leno or Letterman? What comedians do you like? Who do you dislike? What does it mean to sell out?"

Some of those conversations actually took place. My friends Gary Gulman and Bonnie McFarlane and I had a lot of fun talking shop and doing bits with one another. Most of that material went straight to the editing room floor: The producers were much more interested in getting what I called the "Who ate my cookies?" footage.

Like the night I climbed into bed and realized my fan was missing. I knew that the producers were messing with me, setting up a long night of me snoring while my roommates tossed and turned and cursed me. (It didn't happen—instead I yelled at the top of my lungs that I was three minutes away from ripping cameras off the walls. One of the secret elves returned my fan a few seconds later.)

They constantly tried to pit us against one another, encouraging us to form alliances, break alliances, and otherwise partake in all of the reality TV bullshit you've seen before on other shows. Gary, Bonnie, and I did our best not to get involved with any of the drama, sticking to jokes and bits and shoptalk. Alas, not everyone saw it our way. The smell of fame and fortune led the rest of the cast into schemes and betrayals. It broke my heart to see comedians act that way, but this was the nature of the show and I don't blame them for it.

And while I'd like to say that I avoided all the drama out of some noble calling, the truth is that I was terrified of pissing off the wrong person. I didn't know if any of the other comedians knew that I was gay, but I suspected that getting outed in front of millions of viewers was the kind of material that reality TV producers dream of. I kept quiet, didn't make any waves, and was the second person eliminated from the show. I guess when it came down to it, I was still a long way away from being ready for "reality" anything.

CHAPTER 31

THE CORONET (PART TWO)

A brush with death causes Todd to rethink his life (for a few days, anyway).

So I'm in the ambulance, the lights flashing, siren blaring, cutting a path through the traffic on La Cienega. "BLUE FORD TRUCK," the driver says through his PA, his voice full of righteous anger. "MOVE TO YOUR RIGHT, NOW!"

I've got a huge grin plastered across my face. *If this is what having a heart attack feels like, everybody should have one!* Later it will occur to me that the good feelings probably have a lot to do with the gallons of morphine that they've pumped into my system.

They lower me out of the ambulance and wheel me into the emergency room with a definite sense of urgency. A doctor in a white coat strides into the room, looking over my chart. "We have some really good news for you . . . ," he begins.

Your heart just skipped a beat is the way I finish the sentence in my head. *A bit of a scare, but nothing to get concerned about . . .*

"One of our best doctors is on the way. He'll be here in just a few minutes."

Fuuuuuuuck.

This is bad. I mean, what's he supposed to say? "He's not one of our best doctors. In fact, he's a little bit of a drinker. But . . . he's got a great sense of humor and always makes us laugh. You'll love him! You know, just last week he performed open-heart surgery while he was blackout drunk!"

I finally puke. As I'm puking, I can't help but remember one of my brothers telling me that my dad vomited right before he had the heart attack that killed him. I am now officially terrified.

They push me out of the emergency room and down the hall into the OR. We pass Sarah Silverman and Jeff Ross on the way. They seem calm and playful. Maybe I'm overreacting. Still, just in case I'm not, and this is the last time I ever talk to them . . .

"Sarah," I mumble. "If I don't make it, I just wanted to let you know . . ."

"Know what, Todd?"

"Your boyfriend cheats on you."

Later Sarah will confess that even though she put on a brave face in that moment, she was thinking the same thing I was: *This could be the last good-bye.* But you'd never know it from the way she's acting now. "Todd, if you live . . . this is going to be *really uncomfortable.*"

One of Our Best Doctors arrives. His name is Dr. Dohad and goddamn it, he is good, lowering his body to meet me at my level, using that reassuring voice you get from pilots and

Tibetan monks. "Well, it doesn't look like we're going to have to do open-heart surgery . . ."

That's a relief. Then I hear a nurse in the background. "Why are his pants still on?"

A single thought gets stuck in my head, playing and replaying itself in an endless loop: *Just fucking great. I'm having a heart attack . . . and they're going to see my dick. I'm having a heart attack and they're going to see my dick. I'm having a heart attack and they're going to see my dick.*

Couldn't they at least give me a warning, a chance to fluff it up a little bit and make it presentable? I can tell you that "heart attack dick" is worse than pool shrinkage. I was afraid the second my pants were off someone would say, "It says here the patient is Todd Glass . . . Who's the young lady we're operating on?"

I guess morphine has its limits: It works well enough to take my mind off a heart attack, just not so well that it keeps me from worrying that a group of trained medical personnel, who have seen it all and then some, are going to get a glimpse of my dick.

Now it's 4 a.m. They've put a stent into my coronary artery and I'm resting in a recovery room. My friends are still here. So is Chris—he had just arrived at Coachella, fighting his way through who knows how many hours of traffic, when he got the call from Sarah, turned around, and drove straight back to L.A. Somehow he found the time to buy me a flower. But the room is full of people, so he tries to be as casual as he can—which is "not very"—as he awkwardly jams the flower under my pillow.

When everybody leaves I stare at the ceiling for a long time. *I thought that I might be dying and Chris and I couldn't even show our true emotions. What the fuck am I doing? If I die—when I die—how fucking foolish is this all going to seem?*

A few days later, when they wheeled me out of the hospital, I had an epiphany. My senses felt heightened, like I could hear everything: jackhammers, cars, and yeah, the fucking birds were chirping. My eyes began to water. I broke down in tears.

Maybe it's time to rethink my life. I could at least tell a few more friends, right? At least the ones that probably already know. It can't be healthy to live this way.

I looked up at the sun and took a deep breath. Things were going to be different from here on out.

And . . . *scene!* Whatever epiphany I had seemed to disappear a few days later—thinking about change would be as close to change as I was going to get. Aside from replacing cigarettes with Lipitor, I went right back to living the same hidden life as I had before.

NOW
WHAT?

CHAPTER 32

THE BLIND SPOT

Todd comes to terms with his reasons for not coming out.

I met Charlize Theron at a Halloween party. I was dressed like a cop in a very authentic-looking uniform. Charlize pointed to the owner of the house, who had spent maybe $20,000 putting this party together. "Pretend you're a real cop," she said, "and tell him that you're here to shut the party down."

I continued to yank the poor guy's chain for a few minutes, insisting there were a half dozen police cars outside that were ready to shut the place down if he wouldn't. We all got a good laugh out of it when I confessed that the joke was Charlize's idea.

She also knew that I had a new idea for a sitcom and suggested I come by her production company's offices so she could hear the pitch.

Even though we'd already met a few times, I was still really nervous and intimidated. I don't usually get starstruck, but I do get talent-struck, and Charlize has a lot of talent. She greeted me with a hug and a reassuring squeeze.

We sat down in the conference room and I began my pitch: a series of funny situations that revolved around a stand-up comedian in L.A. who is trying to stay in the closet. I told her that it was based on my real life—about Chris and me and our *situation*—and painted a picture with some of the more hilarious things that had happened to us.

When I was done, she told me there was one part that she just couldn't get her head around:

"The audience isn't going to understand why your character is still in the closet. I mean, who really cares anymore? It doesn't make any sense for him to be carrying this secret, especially in Hollywood."

"I know," I tried to explain. "It seems ridiculous, but isn't that what's funny about it? If you're Jewish and hiding in Nazi Germany, that's sad. But if you're Jewish and you're hiding in a synagogue, that's comedy."

"I don't know, Todd. It's not really such a big deal to be gay anymore."

A wave of frustration passed over me. How could she just dismiss everything about my life with one statement? *Not a big deal anymore?* I was angry, but couldn't find the right words to articulate my frustration.

I'd find those words a few months later, thanks to Louis C.K. I was opening up for him on his tour and we had been spending a lot of time traveling together.

"Louis, there's something I want to tell you . . . ," I finally said one night after a show.

"Okay."

"But I can't . . . Can you just say it for me?"

"Uh . . . You're gay?"

"Wait . . . You knew? How did you know?"

"I didn't. But a few minutes ago, when we were talking about how I dealt with the word 'faggot' on my show, you really started to sweat a lot."

We went on to have an amazing conversation. I told him about the meeting with Charlize, eventually getting to the part where she couldn't understand why I'd still be in the closet, especially in Hollywood. Leave it to Louis, a straight guy, to explain my decision with more clarity than I've ever had.

"You didn't start hiding it in L.A.," he said. "You started in Philadelphia, a long time ago. She might be right: Maybe the world has become a little more accepting over time. But you were already comfortable hiding it."

That made perfect sense. The world had changed drastically since I was a kid, but that didn't mean that my original fears were unfounded. Those memories helped to define me. I couldn't just shake them off because people like Charlize thought the world had become a more accepting place. It was great that she'd surrounded herself with open-minded people in an open-minded town, but that wasn't the world I grew up in, or even the world that a lot of other people are still living in today.

There I was, weeks later, finally able to articulate the feelings that led me to leave sweat stains all over Charlize's conference room. I wish I had been able to say all of this to her back then. Instead I got up and said:

"That's a really good point, Charlize. Do you guys validate parking?"

CHAPTER 33

SEPTEMBER 2010

Todd finally finds his motivation.

Five suicides in three weeks.

A nineteen-year-old in Rhode Island who hung himself in his dorm room. The freshman at Rutgers who jumped off the George Washington Bridge. That kid in California, the one who was bullied so much by his classmates that he had to be homeschooled, taunted at a park until he just couldn't take it anymore, who tied a rope to a tree, wrapped it around his neck, and jumped, spending a week in a coma before finally passing on. He was thirteen.

Every one of the kids had a name—Tyler Clementi, Seth Walsh, Raymond Chase, Asher Brown, Billy Lucas. And what about the thousands more whose names I didn't know?

I remember feeling sadness and anger bubbling up inside

of me. Suddenly the struggle with sexual identity didn't feel like a comedic situation anymore. As far as I was concerned, these weren't suicides—the kids might just as well have been murdered by a society that wouldn't allow them to feel comfortable about who they were.

And I wasn't doing a goddamn thing to help.

But what are you going to do, Todd? You're not a politician or a famous actor with a soapbox. You're a comedian. Your job is to make people laugh.

Then I thought about a quote I once heard—I think it was Oscar Wilde who said, "If you want to tell people the truth, make them laugh, otherwise they'll kill you."

I thought about the George Carlin albums I used to listen to when I was the same age as a lot of these kids—albums that were not only hilarious, but filled with sharp insights and social commentary. Carlin always spoke the truth, no matter how controversial it might sound.

Great comedians are truth-tellers. I couldn't even be honest with a lot of my friends about who I was. But when I did tell people, the responses were overwhelmingly positive. When I finally explained to some of my friends that my "friend" Chris, who I'd been dragging back to Philadelphia for the holidays, was actually a lot more than just a friend, they seemed genuinely happy for me.

Still, for weeks after that, I would watch them like a hawk, trying to see if their attitudes toward me had changed. I got the proof I was looking for one day when my old friend Kevin Sousa grabbed a can of soda out of my hand. Ever since hearing those conversations in the '80s about catching AIDS from sharing a drink with someone, I'd been prepared for people to get the willies around me—even reasonably intelligent people might think, *Hey, even if there's just a 1 percent chance, why take the risk?* But—and I swear to God it felt like slow motion—Kevin put the can to his lips and took a giant sip. He didn't ask, he didn't think about it, and he didn't make a comment after he put it back down. I breathed a hundred sighs of relief.

I called my new manager, Alex Murray. "Alex, I feel like I've got to do something. I really think I can bring some clarity to this issue, maybe even get people to see things in a different way."

"What do you mean?"

"Look, I'm not going to change the real homophobes. We're probably just going to have to wait for them to die. But I'm starting to think that they're not even the biggest problem. It's the people who are *mostly* accepting—the ninety-percenters. The people who want to be on the right side of this thing, and really could be, if they just went that last ten percent to help these kids feel awesome about themselves. I grew up with these people. I've been passing as a straight guy for years. I know how they think. I know how to talk to them."

"That's great, Todd. What's stopping you?"

"I don't know. I still don't think I'm ready."

"Maybe you're going to have to do this before you're ready."

Fuuuuck! I knew that he was right. But how the hell was I going to do it?

I know some people who have sat down with a list and called everyone important in their lives, one by one. Others save time and write a group email or make an announcement over family dinner. I also knew that none of those options was for me.

You're not getting off that easy, Todd. You hid it publicly; now you've got to come out publicly.

CHAPTER 34

I'M NOT FUCKING GAY! (BUT I AM.)

WTF?

The ability to shoot cheap video—like we did with *Todd's Coma*—wasn't the only newfangled technological innovation to change comedy. In the mid-2000s, "podcasting" suddenly became a thing.

The first time I did a podcast was my friend Jimmy Pardo's show, *Never Not Funny*. Now listen, if you're reading this and you did a podcast five years before Jimmy Pardo and you're like, "What the fuck, Todd? Why does Jimmy Pardo get all the credit when I started a podcast before him?" Relax. I'm just saying that Jimmy's show was the first time I heard of podcasting.

I instantly loved it. It's easy to see why comedians were attracted to the format—podcasting offered a kind of freedom that wasn't available in a medium like radio. There are a lot of suits in radio. There are a lot of suits in every line of work, but radio always seemed to suffer the most. You could have a number one show for ten years and the suits would still tell you what you could and couldn't do.

I'm not trying to shit on all of the suits in the business. There are a few brilliant ones, maybe 10 percent of them, who should be loved and revered for what they do. But the majority of suits are just like the rest of the world—comfortable with what they already know, looking for a slightly new slant on something that is already recognizable. "It's like *Friends*, but they're forty!"

But if you say, "It's like nothing you've ever heard or seen before," well, a suit is going to have a hard time wrapping his or her head around that concept. The end result? Creativity is going to get stifled, not because the creator lacks imagination, but because the middlemen can't climb inside the creator's mind.

People used to wonder what would happen if they could get rid of the suits. But that's all it ever was—something to imagine—until podcasting came along and answered the question.

It could have been a nightmare. The suits could have had the last laugh. "It's so funny . . . They always thought that they didn't need us, but everything they've done without us has crashed!"

But that isn't what happened. What would happen if we got rid of the suits? Magic, that's what.

I don't think that it's a coincidence that a lot of great comedy podcasts arose from the ashes of failed radio experiments. Scott Aukerman's *Comedy Death-Ray Radio* (now *Comedy Bang!*

Bang!) podcast began in 2009 as part of Indie 103, an incredibly creative and well-regarded radio station that—due to the realities of the industry—had switched to an Internet-only broadcast earlier that year. Marc Maron hatched *WTF* during after-hours at the progressive network Air America, another failed attempt at trying something new on the radio.

Marc's show in particular has become an influential force in the comedy world. He has a way of using his very open neuroses to get other people to talk freely about all kinds of issues in a way that's both honest and hilarious. As I considered all of the vehicles I could use to come out in a public way, I saw *WTF* as a place where I might feel safe enough to actually go through with it. More importantly, his podcast has a big audience, including a lot of the comedians that I work with on a regular basis.

I wasn't sure if I was going to be able to do it more than once.

Leading up to the day, I had doubts that I'd even be able to do it the one time. I was scared shitless. Part of it was my fear of the unknown: I was forty-seven years old—is that really the time in life to shake everything up and hope for the best? Was I really about to let go of the lie that had been with me for my whole life?

How were the people around me going to react? I knew most of my friends were going to be okay with the news, but there were a couple of people—including comedians I love and respect—who had made homophobic comments around me in the past, unaware of my *situation*. How weird and strained were those relationships going to be?

Would audiences respond differently to my jokes? I wasn't

a household name, but I still had a fan base, and they were going to have opinions. It was going to feel mighty strange for complete strangers to know intimate details about my life.

But my biggest fear was that my intentions would be misunderstood: What if people thought that I was coming out publicly as a form of self-promotion?

The day before Marc's show I went for a walk along the beach with my friend Daniel Tosh. I knew that he'd be brutally honest with me.

"I just don't know," I confessed. "Is this a cheesy or a selfish way to do this? Am I going to sound overdramatic?"

"Look, Todd," Tosh said, "not to make you feel bad or paranoid, but people have asked me about you."

"They have?"

"Not like every twenty minutes or anything, but a decent amount. They don't care in the way you think. They mostly feel bad that you feel like you have to hide it from them."

It suddenly dawned on me that hiding who I was from people, especially the ones that already knew, was totally delusional. And self-delusion is not a quality of a good comedian.

I didn't sleep much the night before Marc's podcast. I tossed and turned thinking about what I was going to say and how it was going to come off. I knew I'd only get one shot at it, so it was very important to me that I said everything I wanted to say and not sound angry or bitter.

For the last few weeks I'd been carrying around a piece of notepaper, a place for me to jot down my thoughts about what I was going to say. But the only thing I ever wrote down on it was "Talk about people that knew."

I didn't want the headline the next day to be, "Todd came out on Marc Maron? Big deal, like we didn't already know!" I suspected that, like Daniel Tosh, a lot of people in the comedy business already knew about me.

I reminded myself that I wasn't coming out for these people. This was about the people who didn't know, whose lives might get a little better if they did. And this was about me being completely honest with myself for maybe the first time in my life.

I finally quit trying to sleep. Instead I plowed through It Gets Better videos on the Internet, watching teens and even preteens bravely share their stories. I remember one kid who couldn't have been more than twelve. He was sitting on a bed with his dog, talking into the camera about being gay. *Look at that dog,* I thought. *He doesn't care at all. The dog just loves this kid for who he is.*

I was way too nervous to drive, so my friend Brian offered to give me a ride. It was about a thirty-minute drive to Marc's house. Brian made a few jokes to lighten the mood, but we didn't talk much. I was too busy thinking about how I was about to pull the curtain back on forty years of lies in front of 250,000 listeners.

I walked into the garage where Marc records the show. It was warm and inviting, filled with books—stuffed on shelves, stacked on the floor, crowding the desk where he sits during the interviews. I sat across from him, shifting nervously in my seat . . .

MARC

I have Todd Glass in my garage. We've been exchanging phone calls and he wanted to talk about something and he decided that this was the place to do it and I appreciate that. I don't know if I'd call it a delicate matter, but I thought the phone calls were fun, Todd.

TODD

Oh my God. How long do we make people . . . It's not a big deal. But I was nervous.

MARC

You had a particular . . . You were ready to tell the world something. And I think we should just do it and work back from there.

TODD

That's exactly what I was just thinking as you said it. Because then what we're working toward makes sense.

MARC

There's no reason to drag it all out. But it's interesting . . . [TODD AND MARC PROCEED TO DRAG IT ALL OUT, HEMMING AND HAWING FOR ANOTHER THIRTY SECONDS. FINALLY . . .]

MARC

So what's up, Todd?

TODD

Oh! I just wanted to come on and promote my podcast.

MARC

Oh shit! I had no idea that's what we were doing here.

TODD

Oh yeah! What did you think?

MARC

I thought you were gay!

TODD

Are you shitting me?

MARC

Yeah. Isn't that weird? I'm sorry.

TODD

Oh my God! Did you really think that?

MARC

Yeah!

TODD

Why?

MARC

Because we had these phone calls . . .

Finally, I was ready to break character. And when I say "break character," I mean the role I'd been playing for most of my life.

"Okay, let's cut the shit here. Let me just say this. I have a very hard time saying that. I've always had trouble using that term . . . *Gay?* Fuck that, I'm not *gay*. What the fuck do I have to tell people I'm *gay* for? I'm not fucking *gay*. I'm fucking Todd Glass. I gotta go up to people and tell them I'm *gay*? That's a fucking lie!"

I paused to take a breath, then added: "But it's not."

I don't know what I expected to feel after the show. Relief. Catharsis. But mostly I just felt numb. Marc gave me a sympathetic look. "If you're not ready, and you want me to sit on this episode for a few weeks, that's okay."

"Marc, I've been sitting on this for forty-seven years. Please don't let me stop you."

That night I lay awake in bed again, replaying the interview in my head. Did I say everything I wanted to say? Did I sound articulate? Was I funny? But eventually I realized the most important thing: It was done. The biggest secret of my life was no more.

CHAPTER 35

EVERYBODY'S A COMEDIAN

The comedic community responds to Todd's announcement.

few nights later, I walked into the Improv with my head down.

I've performed hundreds of sets at the Improv. The place that gave me my start in Los Angeles. My home. I've never once walked in with my head down.

But I didn't know what to expect. I felt naked. I was trying not to make eye contact with anyone, but Jeff Garlin spotted me from across the room. "OH MY GOD!" he yelled. "TODD GLASS, MY FAVORITE GAY COMIC!"

I felt a sharp pain in my stomach. *No, Jeff, no!*

But I quickly realized that this was just his way of sending some love my way and reassuring me that nothing had changed. It was great that he was making a joke about it. In a

177

matter of seconds, I went from total embarrassment to absolute relief. I gave Jeff a big hug.

Before I came out, a lot of people told me how big a relief it would be, like a huge weight had been lifted off my shoulders. I knew these people meant well, but I thought that they were full of shit.

Being gay wasn't a plight that I had to get over. I already felt okay with myself. I started to worry that I was going to let everybody down by not having some kind of amazing epiphany.

But then the responses started pouring in. Two days after Marc's podcast dropped, I'd received several hundred emails. Heartfelt messages from friends who were excited to invite me and Chris to stay with them for the weekend. Total strangers telling me how hearing about my situation encouraged them to reexamine the way they were living their own lives. "More power to you," a teenager tweeted at me. "Live the real life."

"Hey, Todd," Jim Gaffigan said. "Just heard your WTF. I'm proud of you. One question: Does your roommate Chris know?"

Jim was joking, but over the next few days I heard from a lot of people who had really believed that Chris was my roommate. *Roommate?* I was in my forties! I hadn't been able to tell people that I was gay, but I was okay with them thinking I had a roommate?

"Hey, Todd, it's Dave," began a voice mail from David Spade. "You really . . . This is not good. This is not going to look good for me. Maybe I can still spin this and make it work. Do you have any black friends? Because maybe if you, me, and a black guy walked around together we could get some press. Call me. You know I'm your friend and as your friend we can fix this."

Jimmy Pardo sent me a text that was short, sweet, and

extremely kind. The next day, when I ran into him at the gym, he shook my hand and leaned in to whisper in my ear, "I can't get AIDS from doing this, can I?"

This is how comedians act sweetly toward one another. Keep in mind that most of us use funerals as a last chance to roast our dear, departed friends.

CHAPTER 36
THE AFTERMATH

Todd embarks on his first year of living openly.

I remember going back to Philadelphia a couple of weeks before coming out on Marc's show. I don't want to make the experience sound too much like a bad movie, where the fate of the hero gets forestalled by some kind of sappy montage, but as I looked around the city, I couldn't help but think: *This is the last time.* My last chance to experience my old life as a (pretend) straight guy. I tried to imagine how my experience was going to be different once everyone knew the truth about me.

The reality—at least as far as Los Angeles was concerned—had been overwhelmingly positive. I couldn't believe how many messages I was getting from complete strangers who'd been affected by my story. Did someone send me a passage from the Bible and call me a sinner? Okay. Did I get a few negative tweets? Sure. But those were the exceptions—almost all of the responses were warm, positive, and kind. I got brilliant emails from kids in high school about how hearing me made them feel a little bit braver about their own *situations*. Others were from people who weren't gay but were living with secrets of their own—a DUI or a drug problem. The details of my story might be different from theirs, but something still resonated with them. It made me feel great that, by doing something healthy for me, I was able to help other people.

But going back to Philadelphia was going to be another story. This was the town where I'd lived with my lie for the longest. There were bound to be uncomfortable encounters with my old friends.

One of the first calls I got was from Tommy Ryan, one of the other Ryans from Smokey Joe's. I remember sweating as I listened to his voice mail. "Hey, Todd," he began in his thick Philly accent, "Tommy Ryan here. Listen, buddy, you had a great run as a straight guy, but let me tell you something: You weren't fooling anybody."

I didn't know whether to laugh or to cry. "Can't wait to fucking see you next week," the message finished. "Love you, buddy."

Tommy's message made me feel great. But as I got ready to do *Preston and Steve,* the morning show I'd done probably a dozen times as a "straight" comedian, my stomach started to ache again.

Preston and Steve had always been one of my favorite shows to do. They move easily between funny and serious, acting incredibly silly one minute, baring their souls the next. But this wasn't like any other appearance I had done with them. We had never talked about something this serious or personal before. There were a lot of different ways my visit could play out.

It couldn't have gone better. For the first forty-five minutes, we talked about my coming out. Then we did another two hours where they didn't mention it once—we did bits, we acted silly, and carried on like none of it made a difference. Everyone associated with the show handled it with so much grace that I didn't want to leave the studio when it was over. The lie was over and done with. I didn't have to be exhausted anymore.

I should add that the next time I went on their show, we didn't get into my sexual identity at all. The time after that, Preston and Steve only mentioned it because they were doing the news and gay marriage came up—giving me the opportunity, for the first time in my entire life, to weigh in on the subject in an honest way. To have people know why I got so emotional when I talked about it. To speak from direct experience, rather than hiding behind the façade of being a particularly open-minded straight guy.

So thank you, Preston and Steve, and Kathy and Casey and Nick and Marisa and everyone else who works on the show. Your acceptance meant the world to me.

I want to reiterate something before moving on to this next part: Coming out has been an incredibly positive experience. It was the right thing to do and not a day goes by where I regret it.

But there have been a few bumps in the road along the way.

I was onstage in Las Vegas when I made a joke about going to the gym. And I could hear some guy mutter from the first row, "That's 'cause you're gay."

I didn't have any time to think about it in the moment. My heart was pounding. I felt miserable. I struggled through the rest of my set without acknowledging that I'd heard the comment. I realized later, in hindsight, that it was the first time someone from the audience had made a disparaging remark toward me that had nothing to do with anything I'd done onstage.

I also decided not to talk about it after the show, when I went out with a group of comedians, because I didn't want to create a situation where people would say, "Oh, so *that's* what it's all about now."

For the first time, I really understood how much it must suck to be that person who's dealing with racism or sexism and gets accused of "pulling a card." Look, do people sometimes bring race or gender into situations where it's just irrelevant? I'm sure that they do. But I'll bet that the majority of the time the feelings are warranted. And I'll bet a lot of those people do exactly what I did that night—I sucked it up and turned inward.

And then there was the radio show in a southern city that I will not name. There are moments, when you're writing a book like this, when you look back on a negative experience and you don't want to give the responsible parties any credit for what they've done. So I'm not going to tell you who these guys are. It's enough to say that these aren't the kind of radio hosts who say things that are poignant or from their hearts. These are the kind of radio hosts who intentionally say stupid, uneducated shit hoping to stir up controversy. Once in a while, they succeed. They know who they are. I like to think that by not mentioning their names, I kind of limit their options to, "Hey, see right here, those dumb guys that he's writing about? It's us!" Or maybe they'll embrace it, handing out copies of the book and telling people, "We're the assholes in chapter 36!"

I had no intention of bringing up my sexuality on their show. My only agenda was to do what I'd done the previous twenty-nine and a half years: be funny.

But they brought it up. One of their very first questions was this: "If you were going to kiss one of us, which one of us would it be?"

Look, if you've ever seen a comedy roast, you know how merciless comedians can be. I can take it and, when necessary, I can dish it out, too. "The truth is," I answered, "I wouldn't kiss either of you ugly motherfuckers. I'm a halfway decent–looking guy with a halfway decent career and, if I'm going to kiss somebody, I'm going to kiss somebody good-looking."

That got a laugh. But they kept going. And going. One dumb question and snide remark after another. Anything can be funny if it comes from an intelligent place. But this situation was in a different area code from anything resembling intelligence. So I stopped being funny and tried to check in with these guys to see where they were coming from.

"Do you think I was born this way?" I asked them. "Do you think this is a choice that I made?"

I actually have to give them credit for what they said next, because at least it was honest. "No," they replied. "We don't think that people are born that way."

Later that night, I was still steaming about the interview. I was talking to a few people after a show, recounting what had happened, when a waiter at the club, a straight guy I'd never met before, said something that really stuck with me. "I get why you want to prove that you were born the way that you are, but who the fuck cares? I'll tell you this: Those guys chose to be un-educated."

I realized he was right. It couldn't have been easy for those guys to ignore so much logic, so many facts and studies. Talk about a fucking choice!

A few nights later I was back in Los Angeles. I'd just done a set at the Improv and was hanging out backstage with a few comics, including Sarah Silverman and Zach Galifianakis. I was telling a story that involved Chris.

"Who's Chris?" Zach asked.

I could feel the familiar ache starting in my belly. "Chris," I said, holding up my fingers to make air quotes, "is my 'friend.'"

And for a second, I felt horrible. *Why couldn't I just have said "boyfriend"? Everything that I've been through over the last few weeks . . . Have I really made any progress at all?*

Until Sarah said, with that adorable way that she says things, "Aw, look at you, Todd . . . You just had a breakthrough!"

Maybe a year from now I'll be able to use the word "boy-friend." Maybe I won't even need the air quotes.

CHAPTER 37

HOW'S LIFE BEEN?

Where Todd keeps working on his act.

The other day I was driving with a friend of mine when he asked me, out of the blue, "Hey, I know this sounds a little campy, but how's life been?"

Not too long ago, Chris and I broke up. Under normal circumstances, I might have kept this private. But given how many lies I've been telling my whole life, I'd like to try to live the rest of it without telling any more. I'm not going to go into all of the details as to why our relationship ended, but I will say that neither of us did anything wrong.

I don't want this to sound like a downer. Of course it's sad when you break up with someone who you've been with for fifteen years, but we're handling it amicably, with love, care, and patience. We even returned to couples therapy for a few sessions to help us remain friends. We still talk all the time. Part of Chris will be in my fiber for the rest of my life, just as I'm sure that part of me will remain in his. I'm not negating the days when we both get depressed, but we should both be proud of the way we're handling this. We lasted longer than most marriages because we did a lot of things right. It's still a journey, but we're headed in the right direction.

I still don't like to use the word "gay." Maybe I'll always have too much baggage associated with it. I don't really like saying that I've "come out of the closet," either. Why couldn't it be something a little more manly, like "stepping out of the garage" or "busting out of the toolshed"?

My act continues to evolve. It started slowly, making air quotes for audiences when I talked about my "girlfriend," earning big laughs from the people that knew. But it was hard to fathom the idea of coming clean in front of a crowd that didn't.

Before a show in Amsterdam last July, my friend Daniel Kinno suggested I talk about it onstage. I was scared shitless. I wasn't ready. But I remembered yet another piece of advice from Louis C.K.: "If you don't feel ready, talk about *that*—talk about not feeling ready." That night, I made another joke about my "girlfriend," adding the air quotes.

But then I kept going.

"The only problem is, I don't really have a girlfriend. I have more of a guyfriend . . . Folks, if I'm not honest about this, Daniel is going to scream at me when I get offstage. So are you all crystal clear on what I'm telling you? I've managed to perform onstage for thirty years without talking about it, so it's a little difficult."

I told a couple of jokes about "busting out of the garage"

and how I preferred the term "partner in crime" to "boyfriend." (What's my crime? *Disobeying God!*) Then I did another hour of comedy that didn't have anything to do with my sexuality. The applause at the end of the show felt great, but it felt even better to realize that, for the first time ever, every single person in the audience knew the truth about me.

Every day I've been reaping the benefits of being honest. Gone are the days of having to tell small lie after small lie until the weight of it all starts to feel like it's going to crush me. My friendships are more honest. If I'm feeling happy or sad about something that happens in my love life, I don't have to tell people that I won the lottery or that I'm upset about an argument I had with my mom.

So how's life going?

Pretty great!

How about you?

How's your life going?

FINAL THOUGHTS.

CHAPTER 38
FINAL THOUGHTS

Because Todd's not quite done talking yet.

I'm guessing that if you've read this far then you're probably already in agreement with some or maybe most of my social views. But I get a lot of emails from all sorts of people with all sorts of beliefs, so I know there are people out there who don't think the way we do. I hope some of these final thoughts will provide you with ammunition to deal with these people in the future. And even if you already agree with most or all of the points I'm hoping to make, sometimes it's important to preach to the choir—it helps us to remember that we're not going through this world alone. We're all in this together.

90 PERCENT ACCEPTABLE

Obviously there will be some people who, no matter what I say here, will never let it sink in and affect them in the way that I hope. I'm talking about openly hateful people who refuse to let go of their preconceived notions and join the rest of us in the twenty-first century. My first choice, of course, is that they change, learn, or evolve past their hate. But if some people can't be helped, maybe all we can do is wait for them to die and hope they don't cause too much damage before they do.

But there is a different group of people who I desperately want to reach out to—the people I like to call the "90-percenters." These are people who consider themselves to be open-minded and forward-thinking individuals but are still, whether they're aware of it or not, hanging on to some last little bit of prejudice or misinformation.

Maybe you're a person who doesn't have a problem with gay people in general, but you still wish that they'd drop the marriage debate. Or, while you don't consider yourself racist—you might have coworkers or even a few friends of different ethnicities—you'd prefer that your kids marry within your own race.

This is a very dangerous line of thought.

A while back I got an email from someone asking me if the fact that they didn't support gay marriage made them homophobic. "I don't have a problem with gay people," the person wrote. "I just don't know why they need to get married. What's wrong with the civil unions?"

First of all, the argument sounds a lot like an "open-minded" person from the 1950s asking why black people need to use the same bathrooms as whites. "Didn't we give them their own bathrooms?" Doesn't sound so open-minded today, does it?

But the fact that you're going to look ridiculous later isn't the dangerous part. When you're 90 percent okay with something, it's easy to convince yourself that your beliefs aren't really hurting anybody else. "Maybe I don't support gay rights," someone might say. "But it's not like I'm tying kids to the back of my truck and dragging them to death." That's true. But the people who do commit this kind of violence aren't necessarily drawing the same distinction between themselves and you. They think of themselves as directly aligned with you and your ideas, and that the major difference between you and them is that you don't have the balls to do what they're doing.

"But Todd, I don't have a problem with gay people—let them do what they want. My son's roommate is gay and he's a great guy. We had him over for Thanksgiving last year. I just wish they'd stop with the marriage thing—that's between a man and a woman." Fine. But do you know what a really homophobic person just heard you say? "Gays aren't equal." That last bit of hesitation on your part might be all the motivation they need to commit a horrible hate crime. And the worst part is that they feel like they're doing it in your name. How does that make you feel?

Now is the time to step up and get to 100 percent. Maybe you're wondering exactly what that means. Shortly after I came out on WTF I got an email from a young father struggling to do right by his son. They were at Home Depot picking out a color to paint his son's room. The kid wanted pink. "Why don't you pick another color?" the father suggested. "Maybe blue? That's a little better for boys."

When the boy refused to change his mind, they scrapped the whole idea and went home. Later that night, his father had a chance to think about what happened. Why does it matter what color he wanted to paint his room? All he was doing was trying to express himself. A really evolved parent would encourage this kind of free expression, not stifle or make him feel bad about it.

Let's be clear: What this father did was far from the worst thing in the world. This wouldn't have been a monumental case of fucking with a child's psychological well-being. But—and this is the part of the story that really resonated with me—why mess with your kid on any level? Why not strive to always be the best, most caring parent you can be, no matter how small the gesture?

To the father's great credit, he went back into his son's room and asked him one more time which color he wanted his room painted. And the best part? Dad was hoping that it was still pink.

Now if you're already there, you should be commended for that. But even if you're at 100 percent, you can still do more. Don't sit quietly and wait for the rest of the world to catch up to you—give the world the help it needs to move along.

Let's say you're at a dinner with your family or coworkers and someone says something—it doesn't have to be overly hateful, but still narrow-minded or prejudiced. Why not correct them?

"Well, because what they just said isn't *that* bad and I really don't want to ruin everyone's night by making a big scene."

But what about the people at that table who are directly affected by those comments? Maybe there are gay people there. Maybe someone has a gay child. Or maybe they're simply evolved, open-minded human beings. How do you think they feel?

I can tell you from experience that standing up for them in that moment would make their night. Don't worry about ruining dinner for someone who doesn't give a second thought about ruining someone's life. It doesn't have to be a big fight that ends the night or a five-hour debate that spoils dinner—a well-placed sarcastic jab will let people know where you stand and make them less likely to make the same comment again, at least when you're around.

"Oh my God, how old *are* you? You sound like you're eighty."

"Hello, the year 1962 called. It wants its social views back."

"Hey, what time is your lynch mob getting together?"

Something I still hear a lot at the dinner table is the old "Is being gay a choice?" debate. Let me give you two quick ways to disarm these people: First, you can simply ask them when they chose to be straight. That one usually stumps them. But if you need more, there's this joke by comedian Danny Bevins: "So if being gay is a choice, that means you can be talked into it, right? I guess you just haven't met anyone persuasive enough."

Believe me, that will do the job.

One last thing: Not everything is clear-cut. We're all on the fence about certain issues. That's okay. Educate yourself. Discuss the issues with your husband or wife, your friends, and the people you trust in your life. Talk to experts who can bring more than just loud opinions to the debate—facts are our friends.

And to whatever extent you can, try to work through your struggles before talking to your kids. Look at it this way: If you're wrong, and they find out (which eventually they will), it will undercut your authority with them for the rest of your life. You probably have plenty of wisdom in other areas to share with them; don't mess it up by getting something so important so wrong.

It's okay if you're not all the way there yet, but can't we let our kids grow up in a world where other people's rights are not up for debate? Let's give them the chance to be a 100-percenter from day one.

THE WORDS YOU "CAN'T" SAY

I was lucky enough to have been surrounded by a lot of warm and kind people who accepted me for who I am with open arms, especially my family. Which kind of begs the question: Why did I stay in the closet for so long?

There are a lot of reasons, but one stands out above all others: From a very young age I continuously heard the word "gay" used as a pejorative term. It was used to express dislike or distaste, a substitute for words like "different," "weird," or "out of the ordinary."

So even though I didn't grow up in a "fuck queers" environment, the seemingly innocuous "gay" remarks have left their scars—the death of my self-esteem by a thousand cuts. And by the way, you don't need a thousand—all you need is to hear it once from someone you respect to leave you apprehensive about your sexuality. I like to use this analogy to help people see my point: It doesn't matter how many times you use an ATM without any problems; you only have to get robbed once to make you scared of using it again for the rest of your life.

That's what happened to me—hearing the word "gay" as

an adjective to describe something in a negative way made me withdraw and hide my secret even deeper. What made it even worse is that these remarks often came from people who considered themselves open-minded, forward-thinking individuals who would argue that their use of the word "gay" didn't represent any ill will toward people who were actually gay. These people would never go up to a gay person and say, "Hey, fag!" But for some reason they desperately want to convince you that somehow there is a difference between doing that and using "gay" as a shorthand for "weird" or as the punch line of a joke. I like to take these people down memory lane. It wasn't too long ago that a lot of good people made similar distinctions between calling someone a "nigger" or "kike" and using terms like "nigger-rig" and "Jew me down."

I've got to admit that in my lifetime we've come a long way. Using the word "gay" as a punch line or a pejorative isn't nearly as acceptable as it used to be. But there are still similarly contentious words in our lexicon today. I learned my lesson early in my career when I made an easy joke about a waitress who dropped a tray of drinks while I was in the middle of my act. "Oh, I see we've got one of Jerry's Kids waiting tables tonight!" It was a hacky joke I'd heard countless times, one that played on the widely accepted stereotype that Jerry's Kids are clumsy people who can't do things the right way. The joke got a laugh and I moved on. Fortunately, not everyone else did: A comedian by the name of Dwayne Cunningham took me aside after the show.

"Look, Todd, Jerry's Kids aren't stupid or slow. They have muscular dystrophy. They aren't clumsy because they're not paying attention. It's a physical disease."

You want to know the funniest part about what I said? I was taking an ignorant shortcut. Sometimes it seems easier to use stereotypes to get a point across. Instead of saying "clumsy," "cheap," or "lazy," we look for a group that, for whatever reason, has been identified as clumsy, cheap, or lazy. Not only is this practice offensive, but—when you stop to think about it—it's not a shortcut at all. It's way more work. JUST USE THE ADJECTIVE! It will save you time and effort.

There are many reasons why we use certain words in certain ways. But how and why you chose to use these words in the past is irrelevant here. Once someone educates you or makes you look at something from an angle you weren't privy to before, it's on you to evolve.

It's a situation I see a lot with "retarded." You don't have to be a language scholar or an anthropology professor to figure out why you should stop using the word. All you need is a little empathy to figure out that using any word that defines someone else's existence in a pejorative way is wrong.

"Not so fast, Todd—what if I'm referring to someone who is actually mentally challenged"? Well, why not use "mentally challenged"? There are a lot of medical terms used to describe this particular condition—let's use the ones that they, their doctors, and their caregivers use.

Yes, you might find some loopholes that let you continue down the path you're on now, especially if you're really looking for them. But why do that? Why try so hard to hang on to something that won't stand the test of time and, in the meantime, is hurtful toward other people? How long are you going to wait before you decide to evolve? Do you really have to say "retarded" at a party and have everyone stare at you in disbelief for you to get that it's over? I'm not talking about supersensitive, politically correct Hollywood liberals—I'm talking about your friends who simply evolved faster.

Or as one of my listeners, Andrew McClain, pointed out in an email: "I just want to give a big shout-out to all the supercool, courageous men and women who still call things *retarded*. Keep fighting that fight—any ridicule that you'll face will be worth it, I promise. History will remember you as brave and principled warriors of free speech."

What do you do when you're around people who still use these terms? It isn't always easy to correct them—many of them love to act like indignant victims of an unfair prosecution:

"What are you, the Word Police?"

No, I'm not the Word Police. I just know something you don't. Let me put it a different way: If you want to pull down your pants and take a shit in the middle of a crowded mall, that's your business. But what you can't do is look at the shocked and appalled people around you like there is something wrong with *them*. And you certainly can't get offended if someone politely points out that there is a bathroom nearby. They aren't the Shit Police—they're just trying to do the right thing.

Sometimes I like to blindside people with analogies. I used to be a big fan of hypotheticals: "So you want to use the word 'retarded' to mean 'clumsy'? Well, how would you feel if instead of 'retarded,' we used 'woman'?"

The problem with hypotheticals, however, is that they usually don't work. They're gimmicky. People know that you're using them to make a point. When you're dealing with a stubborn person—someone who insists on using "retarded" in a certain context despite efforts to persuade them otherwise—the hypothetical is going to seem like a full-frontal attack.

So you have to blindside these people. Go into secret agent mode. Let them think you're on their side. "I'm not the Word Police," you can assure them. "I think it's so funny that you say 'retard' whenever someone drops something. In my house, when I was growing up, we just used 'woman'" (or "bald" or "Mexican" or whatever adjective describes the person you're talking to— you get the point).

Immature? Maybe a little. But if you make it subtle and play it real, I guarantee that eventually you'll get through to them.

A good rule of thumb, whenever you're in doubt as to what a group of people should be called, is to just call them whatever THEY want to be called. Sure, sometimes members of a particular group will adopt the slurs used to describe them and try to take the sting out of them by using these words to describe themselves. Trust me when I tell you this: That's their second choice. If it was up to them, they'd rather that word didn't exist or was never used in a negative way in the first place. Since that's not an option, they've found the second-best way to deal with it.

All of this is especially important if you're a parent. I can almost guarantee you that your kid will hear the word "retarded" used to put someone down, but does he really have to hear it from you?

So you can make the call now and spare yourself the embarrassment down the road. Evolution isn't just a favor to society; it's a favor to yourself.

NOBODY IS COOL WITH EVERYTHING

I was having a conversation with friends one night when somebody brought up the idea of having a father who was transgender. As I started to play this hypothetical situation out in my mind—imagining my dad, dressed as a woman, coming to one of my shows, being introduced to my friends—I think I surprised everyone there—especially me—when I confessed that I would probably be uncomfortable.

There's part of me that's embarrassed to admit that I'd be embarrassed. I've spent a lot of this book preaching tolerance, and it's difficult for me to recognize that I might not be the 100-percenter I hope to be.

But I'd like to think that I would be self-aware enough to realize that the problem didn't lie with my hypothetical cross-dressing dad, but with me. That I wouldn't try to convince him to hide or change who he was just so I would feel more comfortable. That I would seek professional help and learn how to have a kind, caring relationship with him just the way he is. That I would recognize and admire his courage to be himself and hopefully even learn from it.

We're all confronted with people and situations that take us outside of our comfort zones. Sometimes they can be a lot to deal with. But if you can recognize that maybe the problem isn't what the other person is doing, but rather the way you are responding to it, then you'll be helping to create a world that's more comfortable for everybody.

"HI, GLENN!"

I notice a lot of people get upset about what I call "fake arguments." One of my favorite ones is the so-called War on Christmas—"You can't even say 'Merry Christmas' without someone jumping down your throat!"

Let's say you own a store, and one of your employees insists on saying, "Hi, Glenn!" to everyone who walks in:

"Hi, Glenn!"

"Hey there, Glenn!"

"Good morning, Glenn!"

This might not bother you. The employee is taking the time to be friendly, and most people, even if they're a little confused, will accept "Hi, Glenn!" as a nice gesture and move on with their day. But would you be wrong to correct your employee? "You might not want to say 'Hi, Glenn!' to everyone, because not everyone is named Glenn. You can just say 'Hi,' can't you?"

And how ridiculous would your employee seem if he snapped back at you? "That's bullshit! You can't even say 'Hi, Glenn!' anymore!"

Of course you can . . . if you're talking to Glenn.

As a Jew, I really don't mind if someone wishes me a Merry Christmas. I appreciate the sentiment. But "Happy Holidays" is a way of expressing the same sentiment that tries to include everybody—it's not a provocation to war.

EMPATHY IS NOT A COMPETITION

Pick any point in history and you're going to find a group of people who are fighting for equality. But the details of each plight are different, leading some people to insist that you don't compare their movement to yours.

I've heard some people say, for example, that you can't compare being gay to being black, because being gay is something that you can hide. Yes, that particular aspect of the struggle is much easier for gay people. But how about the fact that if you're black the whole world might be against you, but at least you don't have to worry about your parents hating you as well? You've got to admit that the gays have a tougher time in that regard, don't you?

After my WTF episode, a lot of people reached out with their stories. I met a guy after a show who started to tell me that he felt like he knew what I had been through because he had a drug problem that he hid for a very long time. Then he stopped himself. "I don't mean to compare what I went through with what happened to you . . ."

It was my turn to stop him, to let him know that it was okay to continue. He was just trying to relate to me. It didn't matter how he was trying to do it. All that matters is the act of compassion. When someone is standing in front of you, trying to relate with you, don't let how they do it get in the way of the fact that they're doing it.

Can we just agree that empathy is not a competition? Yes, some people have a harder struggle than others, but isn't the ultimate goal to not struggle at all?

THE REAL WORLD IS SAFER THAN A SCHOOL BUS

You already know that I had a hard time at school. That's why when I talk to friends who have kids in school today I'm so happy to hear about all the progress we've made. Sure, bullying remains a big problem, but I think our schools are trying to take great strides toward creating a safer and more nurturing environment for everyone.

That's why I am so sick and tired of hearing some people say that we pamper and protect kids in schools too much today and that it doesn't prepare them for the "real world."

I'm not a child psychologist, a teacher, or even a parent, so my expertise in certain areas is obviously limited. I can't tell you, for example, why giving out trophies to every kid just for participating is a good idea. But as someone who grew up with a learning disability, I consider myself an expert in just how fucking tough school can be. Kids can be cruel and merciless. So can some adults.

As much progress as we've made, chances are that a ten-year-old kid is much more likely to get harassed, made fun of, or bullied during a walk from the front to the back of the school bus than he or she would be walking five blocks in New York City. So the idea that all this "pampering" won't leave kids prepared for the real world is bullshit: The real world can often feel like a much safer place than a school bus full of bullies.

WE'VE NEVER GIVEN RIGHTS AND REGRETTED IT LATER

The national conversation over gay marriage rages on. Once again we find ourselves in a debate over giving equal rights to yet another group of Americans.

I can't fucking believe that we're having this conversation again. We've been in this place time and time before. How is it possible that it still requires a national dialogue? When, in the history of this country, have we ever given rights to a group of people and—once we've had time to adjust to the change—regretted the decision later?

Never.

Not once.

Maybe you disagree with me on this. If there is a group whose rights to equality you wish we could take back, I beg you to bring it up the next time you're at a party or on a date.

Let me know how that goes over.

PAIN AND GAIN

A few years ago I was walking down the street with my friend Gary Gulman when we saw a group of high school kids getting into a limo on their way to prom. I spotted a gay couple among them. My first instinct was to feel a little sad.

"Look at that," I said to Gary. "I wish I got to go to prom. I mean, I'm not complaining. I guess all of the things that happened to me made me who I am today. More empathetic. A better comedian . . ."

But then I had a second thought: *FUCK THAT!*

Growing up with learning disabilities—and, later, my *situation*—didn't make me a funnier comedian or a better person. I just did the best I could with the hand I was dealt. And I was one of the lucky ones, born to good parents and surrounded, for the most part, by kind and smart people.

I think it's great when people manage to use hardship and pain as a source for inspiration to help others or make this world a better place. But it's not a necessary part of the process. Trust me: We'll still have music, movies, and art even if people aren't bullied when they're kids. Life will give you plenty to deal with before it's over—whether it's lost loves, unexpected deaths, or other misfortunes. You'll have all kinds of opportunities to learn from pain. I just don't think it's necessary to inflict it on each other on purpose.

GEORGE CARLIN

If you've listened to my podcast (*The Todd Glass Show*—available for download on iTunes!) you probably know that I'm a huge George Carlin fan. "I swear to George Carlin" is what we say when we want to let one another know that we're telling the absolute truth. A lot of listeners have kindly suggested that Carlin—who famously said that "there are no bad words"—would have mocked me for having a problem with words like "fag" or "retarded."

What you have to remember is that George Carlin grew up in an era where people were offended by Elvis's crotch instead of, say, segregation or any of the other social wrongs of the time. When he talked about people getting offended by certain words, he wasn't talking about the ones who would rather you didn't use the word "faggot" or "retard" just because you weren't smart enough to use the proper adjective. He was talking about the hypocrites who look the other way when it comes to the major wrongs being done in this world and instead choose to get offended at less meaningful things.

And by the way, I don't really get offended when I hear these words. I get . . . confused. When I hear someone use "retard" to mean "stupid" or "gay" to mean "feminine" or "different," to me it's like watching someone light a cigarette on an airplane or drink a beer while driving. I'm not offended, it just looks wrong. If anyone gets offended, it's mostly these people after you correct them. Their feathers get ruffled and they choose to concentrate on what their ego is saying instead of their brain. They get offended, but at the wrong thing. I think that's an idea that would have been okay with George Carlin.

He always managed to be ahead of his time in his day, and I suspect that, if he were still with us, that would still be true.

BACK THEN

I'm exhausted with people who say how great things used to be . . . back then.

Back then a marriage was between a man and a woman. *Back then* families stayed together. *Back then* people were more polite, better dressed, and had cleaner haircuts.

I get why some people might think it was better, but it wasn't. Most of the problems we have today existed "back then." Those family photos that look so perfect? They were staged. The big difference between then and now is that then, instead of trying to deal with the problems openly, people tried to sweep them under the rug.

"My husband is an alcoholic . . ."

"Shhhh!"

"My wife was raped . . ."

"Shhhh!"

"My mother is suffering from depression . . ."

"Shhhh!"

"My daughter married a black guy."

"Shhhh!"

"My son is gay . . ."

"Double shhhh!"

As Mr. Rogers used to say, "If it's mentionable, it's manageable." Back then they didn't mention much, so how manageable could life have really been? The term "unmentionables" was born out of people not being able to mention their underwear. How was a society that couldn't even talk about *underwear* going to tackle massive social inequality?

Let me tell you something else: The world we live in today is the way it is because of how things were back then. If everything back then had worked the way some people seem to believe that it did, we never would have stopped doing those things.

"Back then we had prayer in school!" Sure. We also failed to account for alternative religious beliefs and left a lot of kids feeling alienated and confused. And by the way, if your kid wants to say a prayer before class, no one is stopping them. These people who complain about there being no prayer in school are perpetuating a fake argument. All we did was make religion in school more inclusive for everyone. I think your God would be okay with that.

"Back then parents stayed together!" Maybe the divorce rate was lower, but there were a lot more unhappy marriages, forcing some kids to grow up in homes filled with resentment, hate, and violence.

"Back then there wasn't as much violence on TV!" No, you couldn't watch *The Sopranos*. Meanwhile, in real life, the Holocaust was happening.

"Back then a man would open a door for a lady and always pay for dinner." Yeah, they also didn't want women to work or vote. That's a trade-up!

Another problem with these Back Then people is that if you ask most of them how far back they want to go, it's always to the day after they got their rights, but the day before somebody else got theirs. Next time you hear people saying things were better back then, ask them what year they would like to go back to. Then ask them to take a selfless look at where other people's rights were at that time. Can we agree that maybe it wasn't better for *everybody* back then?

Obviously most of the Back Then people are older. Some people will tell you that old people have a "get out of jail free" card because of their age. They grew up in a society that was racist, sexist, or homophobic, and we shouldn't expect them to change now. "My grandma is really old," you might say. "Doesn't that excuse some of the racist things she sometimes says?"

I think my friend Eric Ohlsen put it best when said, "Oh really? Is your grandmother older than Abraham Lincoln?"

I remember something my uncle once told me: "You can't have the benefits of a forward-thinking society *except* when it comes to your prejudices." So you really want to go back to the way things were? Let's start by handing over your Lipitor, turning off your air-conditioning, and throwing away your cell phone.

What's that? You don't want to go that far back? I see—you want to go back to the day when you didn't have to be an open-minded, accepting human being. You want all the advancements that come with modern society except the ones that will require you to change your bigoted, outdated views.

I get that it's a lot harder for older people to change their views. Most of them probably won't. But some people learn, evolve, and change late in life and that is extraordinary. So if you want to use your age as an excuse to dig in on your positions, go right ahead—no one will blame you. But what you're basically saying is that you are not extraordinary. I wouldn't brag about that.

An evolved person doesn't want to go back to a time that was better for him or her, but forward to a time that can be better for everybody.

MACHINES DON'T HAVE EGOS

While we're on the subject of technological advancements, it's true we're doing pretty well. Cars, planes, cell phones, the Internet—we've come a long way in a very short period of time.

What's interesting is how technology progresses so much faster than society. There's still a debate over whether or not homosexuality is an illness that can be cured, even though psychiatrists have been telling us otherwise since 1974. Why can technological innovation happen so quickly while social innovations seem to take forever?

The answer is simple—people have egos, machines don't. If cars had egos and refused innovations and new ideas the way some stubborn people do, we'd all still be driving cars with wooden wheels and no air bags. Changing a person's point of view is fucking difficult.

When deciding what dishwasher to buy, people tend to base their decisions on what the experts say. With social issues it's often the opposite—people look for "experts" who will support their already existing point of view.

All I'm asking for is consistency. It drives me crazy when someone who believes in an archaic practice like "conversion therapy" to address homosexuality uses the Internet to find a place to take their kid, belts them into their brand-new car loaded with the latest safety features, and uses their smartphone to look up directions. You're willing to do all of that and still entrust a child's mental well-being to someone without any scientific credentials who wants to "cure" him or her with a set of two-thousand-year-old beliefs? That's selfish, plain and simple.

Next time your car breaks down or your heart starts beating irregularly, don't go to a mechanic or a hospital—go to the same person you go to for your social beliefs. Let your archaic views ruin your life in the same way they are ruining everyone else's.

BEING GAY ISN'T HEROIN

Every day in this country, gay kids are thrown out of their own home because their parents don't accept them for who they are. This is often called "tough love."

It's not.

If your child is on drugs, there are plenty of therapists or counselors who will tell you to turn them away. If you let them live in the house, feed them, and give them money, you may only be supporting their addiction. Some people need to hit rock bottom before they can face an addiction; kicking them out of the house can sometimes help them get to that place a little faster. That's "tough love."

When professional drug counselors recommend tough love, they do so because of extensive research and past results. They know it can work. And if it doesn't and your child dies before getting better, no one will blame you for making the choice that you did. You might blame yourself, but you will have plenty of professional help from people who will reassure you that you did the right thing.

Some parents take the same approach toward their gay children. But consider this: If you cut off contact with your gay child and he or she commits suicide, no one is going to come to your defense. There aren't going to be a lot of people saying you did the right thing. You might hear some words of compassion and people might tell you to forgive yourself but that will take a lot of work on your part. You'll have to learn the hard way and maybe you'll be able to heal by helping other people in your situation avoid making the same mistake you did.

But wouldn't it be easier to just skip all that and love your children for who they are while they're alive?

LOOK FOR THE HELPERS

At times, especially when I start ranting, I can sound like a pretty negative person. I'm not. One of the greatest things about coming out has been the volumes of messages I've received that remind me just how decent and kind people can be. Things are getting better. People are doing great things. Let's take a moment together to acknowledge that.

I want to leave you (okay, I don't really want to leave you, but here we are at the end) with something else that the late Fred Rogers once said. By pretty much every account, Mr. Rogers was one of the great ones, someone whose humanity and decency were evident to anyone who spent time with him. It's easy to look back at Mr. Rogers now and see a guy in a cardigan who wouldn't have had any clue as to how to address the social problems we face today. But I don't think that's true. "When I was a boy and I would see scary things in the news," he said, "my mother would say to me, 'Look for the helpers. You will always find people who are helping.'"

Thanks, Fred.

And thank you.

Good night.

CHAPTER 39

A LETTER TO MOM AND DAD

As I said earlier in the book, it took a series of teenage suicides to open my eyes to how devastating hatred can be to a child. I still feel the urge every day to speak up for those kids, making sure that the people who surrounded them understand their complicity in those tragedies and maybe helping others avoid a similarly heartbreaking set of circumstances.

Let's face it—most of the people I want to address would never read this book. But they might respond to a heartfelt plea from the kids who need them.

The following letter is mostly made up of passages from the book, so if I sound like I'm being repetitive, well, yes, I am. My hope is that it might help someone articulate the feelings he or she is (literally) dying to express to a parent who wouldn't in a million years read a book by a gay, dyslexic comedian.

Dear Mom and Dad,

These might not be my words, but I hope that what you're about to read helps to explain the way I'm feeling right now. It's important that you know I want nothing more than what any other kid on this planet hopes for: to be loved and accepted by his or her parents. But your actions have prevented me from living that kind of life everyone around me gets to enjoy. You have taken that from me. Stolen that from me. But I want you to know that it's not too late and I beg for you to give this letter serious thought.

Ever since I was little, you've made me feel bad about myself. Now you've chosen to turn your back on me completely. I get that me being gay is not what you wanted. Believe me, if I had a choice I would gladly change this about myself if for no other reason than to end this nightmare.

But I can't. And I wish you could put half as much effort into understanding and loving me as you have into trying to change me.

I'm sure you have your reasons. Maybe it has to do with your religious beliefs. But from my point of view, the idea that you would let an archaic institution separate you from your child doesn't make any sense to me (or to most people who know anything about these things). I know you think they're right about me, but they're not. Besides, why would you trust and follow "experts" who make your life easier while choosing to ignore the ones who could make my life easier?

Maybe you think I'm sick. Well, you'll be hard-pressed today to find a pediatrician or an accredited psychologist who will tell you that homosexuality is an illness. In fact, any doctor who diagnosed homosexuality as a mental illness would be discredited by every medical board in the country. Shouldn't that alarm you? Don't you trust doctors to fix your health problems, plumbers to fix your sink, or mechanics to fix your car? There are people who dedicate their entire professional careers to understanding what we're going through—why can't you listen to what they're telling you? Why do you instead trust my well-being with people with no academic background or experience?

I get what you think you're doing. If I were on drugs there would be plenty of counselors who would tell you to turn me away just like you've done now. They would tell you that by letting me in your house, feeding me, or giving me money, you will only be supporting my addiction. That I may need to hit rock bottom before I can really begin to change.

But do you know why a professional therapist or counselor might make this kind of recommendation? Because of their extensive research and past results. They know it can work. And if (God forbid) I was to die from an addiction before getting better, no one would blame you for making that choice. Even if you blamed yourself, you would have plenty of professional help from people who could reassure you that you did the right thing.

But guess what? I'm not on drugs or engaging in illegal or dangerous behavior. I'm gay. And if something was to happen to me, no one will come to your defense for cutting me out of your lives. No one will tell you that you did the best thing. That's not an opinion; that's a fact. Maybe some people will tell you to forgive yourself eventually but that will be a long road. You'll have to educate yourself, learn from your mistakes, and maybe use your example as a warning to other parents in your shoes.

But wouldn't it be easier to just skip all that and love me for who I am for as long as I'm alive?

I think, deep down, you know that there is nothing wrong with me; the truth is I'm different than what you were expecting and you don't know how to deal with it. I know it's hard for you to accept me because so many people in your social circles are telling you not to. I imagine it must be embarrassing to have a gay child when those around you still think being gay is "weird." I can't change. You can, but don't want to. And that's what hurts the most.

I want to end this on a positive note. Like I said, it's not too late. I don't want to hold on to anger or any feelings of resentment. Even though some of the points in this letter might sound harsh, I love you very much and hope that you'll learn to accept me for who I am.

Love,
[Fill in your name here.]

ACKNOWLEDGMENTS

MOM

Kids are usually embarrassed to discover that they get their sense of humor from their parents—especially their mothers. But as an adult I can totally see it. I am very proud to have received that from you, Mom. I think every parent wants to hear that they did a good job and I just wanted you to know that you did. As my brother Michael put it, "I like who I am because of you."

DAD

Well, it wasn't until I got older that I realized how much of you is in my fiber, Dad. I miss you. I love you. I think about you more and more often as the years go on. I just smelled your sweater yesterday. You did a good job, too.

MY BROTHERS

Like most families, we are not without problems, but our family drama is normal family drama. I'm not saying we take each other for granted, but we often don't take the time to express how we feel about one another. A few years ago my brother Spencer put it perfectly when he said, "We all really like each other." Whenever we all get together, we can count on laughing a lot—I don't know that a lot of families can say that. So thank you, Spencer, Michael, and Corey.

THE REST OF MY FAMILY

Thanks to Katy and Tyler—not only are you my niece and nephew, but as you've gotten older, you've become my friends. Meryl . . . I realize that for a lot of years I might have taken you for granted, but that's only because you fit into our family so seamlessly. You always felt like a sister to me. I love your great energy and am always excited to see you. Wendy . . . You don't talk that much and you keep things simple. I love you for that. Erin and Sammy . . . next time I'm home I'll take you to Target again and we'll get Slurpees. Steve . . . You can be sillier than all of us—that is a bonus. Thanks for the rides to and from the airport, the five trips a day to Wawa with me, and for putting dimmer switches on all the lights so I'm comfortable. Little Steve . . . thanks for laughing at all my jokes. Cara . . . thanks for laughing and giggling and keeping my mom busy.

CHRIS

There's so much I want to say and I don't know where to start—it's taken me a half hour at my desk, starting and stopping and starting and stopping again, just to get this far. I hope that, in reading this book, you know the way that I feel about you. Because of you I did and saw things that I never would have done or seen without you. It may have seemed like I complained a lot: "It's too hot . . . I don't want to see the Eiffel Tower." But if you were a fly on the wall, you'd hear me talking about those trips all of the time—the family dinner in Italy, visiting your dad in Bangkok, camping in your old VW van. Then there's your constant and never-ending belief in me and support for my career. Although our relationship may be different now, I know that our journey, our friendship, and our love for each other will continue to grow.

CHRIS'S FAMILY

I guess you could say with Chris I got lucky twice—once with Chris, once with his family. They *knew* before either of us was ready to admit our relationship and treated me like I was part of the family. I remember once hearing one of the nieces referencing me as her uncle—I've got to tell you, it made me melt. So thank you, Pierrette, Henry, Sam, Annalisa, Sibonne, Mike, and Stephanie!

THE ANONYMOUS BENEFACTOR

I already mentioned it in the book, but to the anonymous benefactor who paid for me to go to Wordsworth Academy: This was the most decent, kind, and selfless gesture that has ever been put in front of me. Even though you remain anonymous to this day, I hope you know how much it meant to me.

STEVE YOUNG

From the time you saw me in line to see a show and told the doorman not to charge me, you have treated me like a member of your family. Whether it was giving me spots or helping me move to L.A.—where you drove me around, something I couldn't fathom doing myself—you took me under your wing and nurtured my comedy. I'm not exaggerating when I tell you that I think about that a lot. You did so much to help me become a good comedian, from booking the great comics I got to see at your clubs to teaching me that the audience isn't always right. These were valuable lessons I never forgot. I'm sorry I haven't told you that enough.

JOY LITTLE

From the time I started working Comedy Works—I was just seventeen—you were like my comedy mom. And even though you're gone now, I think of you always, which is not hard to do since your face is the wallpaper on my cell phone. I think about how kind you were and how great it felt to make you laugh— especially the time I got out of the car on the Schuylkill Expressway and started dancing. Watching you convulse with laughter was the best feeling in the world. You are missed.

ANDY SCARPATI

It started as a professional relationship and quickly grew into a friendship. And I've never told anyone this before, but it was a friendship that grew into love and a secret love affair. I should have stayed in Philly and married you, Andy . . . Okay, just kidding. This joke was just for you. You had such a great energy that I was always looking forward to seeing you, no matter what we did together. I love you and thank you for all the help and support early on.

THE JONESES

I think about your family all the time. No matter how many years have passed, I always remember what a kind thing you did for me when I was a nervous kid moving out to L.A. Being welcomed so warmly into your home helped a lot. I look back on that time with genuine fondness and appreciation. So Caroline, Randy Jr., Randy Sr., and Sue . . . What can I say? Thank you.

THE HELFRICHES

When the Joneses moved, Martha's mom, Mim, invited me to stay with them—rent free—which allowed me to concentrate on doing comedy full-time. We sat on those sofas and talked and talked—you may be the only person I've ever met who can talk as much as me. I cherish those memories. So thank you, Mim. I miss you.

LYNN AND TERESA SHORE

When I came out to Lynn and Teresa a long time ago, they confessed that they'd always had a feeling. "Buddies don't let each other drive their cars," Lynn chuckled. That line made me laugh so hard I remember it to this day. You are so special to me. Our time together is precious to me. I am so lucky to have you as friends. So thank you and let's hang out more.

DR. DOHAD

I'm a little embarrassed I didn't send this to you a long time ago, but you know what they say: Better late than never. I remember lying in the hospital when you walked in for the first time, leaned down over my bed, and reassured me that I didn't need open-heart surgery. That was the best news I had gotten that night and you made me feel at ease. Thank you for saving my life.

PODCAST CREW

The people that work on *The Todd Glass Show* with me have become my second family. So thank you, Chris Burden (you funny fuck), Katie, Mikey, Andrew, Eric, Jingle Joe, Jake Adams, Preston Smith, Aristotle, and, of course, Tom Martin and Blake Wexler. Besides stand-up comedy, doing the show is my favorite thing in the world. Thanks also to Chris Hardwick for letting me do whatever I want and never calling me with instructions.

LINDA WASDEN

You're like the best aunt in the world. When this is all over, and you know what I'm talking about, we are going to party like crazy people. Be strong. Love, Todd.

HOWARD STERN

I've always admired Howard Stern—his show is real, honest, and in the moment. Growing up, he made my friends and me laugh so hard we would LITERALLY have to pull off the road. When I started doing my podcast, I wanted to do a similar type of show, but quickly realized that getting honest on the air meant I had to come clean about a few things in my life. Hiding my sexuality might have been acceptable onstage—where I could find other truths to talk about—but it wasn't an option for the podcast. Still, it took me a year to come out in a public way. I can't tell you how nervous I was to come back and do my show after my announcement, or how happy I was to realize that nothing had changed for the worse. In fact, the show was much better—we could finally incorporate my *situation* into bits, talk honestly about serious issues, and make all kinds of new jokes I couldn't have before. My listeners responded with comments that were warm and reassuring and emails that went deeper and more openly into things we talked about on the show. So thank you to all my listeners, and thank you, Howard. You set the standard for honesty on the air so high, it pushed me into the right direction on my show and in my life.

KEVIN AND PATTI SOUSA

Listeners to my podcast know him as Almost-Dr. Kevin Sousa—although by the time this book comes out, the "Almost" part will be gone. I've known you, Kevin, since I lived in Philadelphia. You were instrumental in helping me make the decision to come out: A week after I told you I was thinking about it, you called me to find out what progress I'd made. When the answer turned out to be "not much," you pushed me to call Marc Maron. Your kindness, love, and professional therapeutic skills helped me get through the scariest thing I've ever done. I hope you know how I feel about you. And while we're talking about the Sousas, thank you to Patti—your love has always meant a lot to me, especially around the holidays—and to the rest of the family: Jon, Terry, Peter, and Michael.

MARC MARON

I knew it then, but time has proven over and over again that I picked the best person I could have to tell my story to. You combine twisted humor and smart, serious conversation in a way that made what should have been a terrifying experience into one that was actually very enjoyable. I was so nervous walking into that garage I felt nauseous. But you put me in such a comfortable place that those feelings quickly disappeared. I got to say everything I wanted to say, the way I wanted to say it. So Marc, what can I say? Thank you.

JEFF ROSS

I used to say Jeff Ross sort of saved my life, but then realized that I didn't need to add "sort of." Jeff Ross saved my life. When he called an ambulance for me that night at the Coronet, I thought he was going to look silly afterwards. He didn't. The doctor told me that because I got to the hospital so quickly there was no damage to my heart. So Jeff, thank you—I wasn't ready to stop doing comedy just yet.

JIMMY KIMMEL

I've always loved watching Chris Elliott on *Letterman*—he does irreverent pieces that are like nothing I've ever seen on any other show. I know it takes a huge amount of trust in someone to let them do whatever they want. Well, that's what Jimmy Kimmel has done for me. I've never been on a show that has given me such an extraordinary amount of freedom, and that takes a tremendous amount of confidence. I don't take this for granted. So thank you. I also want you to know that Uncle Frank lives on with my nieces, my nephews, and my friends. That said, you're lucky you're even getting a mention here, since I haven't been on the show in a fucking year.

DAVE BECKY

Dave, you probably don't know this, but you are the first person in the comedy community I told about my situation. The reason it was you was because you always said extremely kind, loving things that made me comfortable enough to trust you with it. At a time when I felt like I was going to burst if I didn't share it with someone, it gave me a lot of comfort to be able to share it with you. Thank you.

MY FUNNY FRIENDS

Steve Rosenthal, thank you for being so supportive, helping me to take ideas that are in my head and bring them to fruition—especially *Todd's Coma*. Thanks also, Mike Koman, because if he reads this he'll get upset. But really it's directed at Steve. Also Jimmy Dore, Stef Zamorano, Dave Rath, Erin von Schonfeldt, Mark Anderson, and Darrin McAfee—these people are practically family, but there's more to it than that: Your never-ending kindness, love, and support remind me that I'm funny. Your presence in my life is appreciated; I wanted to make sure that you knew it.

ALL THE COMICS*

Whenever I know that I'm about to hang out with comedians, I feel like a little kid ten feet away from Disneyland. Whether you're a comedian I used to work with every week at the Improv or someone that I worked with one time five years ago in Minneapolis, I cherish our time together. I feel so lucky to be a part of this crazy fraternity. So thank you for making life fun and for helping to create a place for grown-ups to act like adolescent kids (while getting paid for it!).

---

*This page is brought to you by . . . *The Bitter Buddha*. (A great documentary about Eddie Pepitone, directed by Steven Feinartz.) Eddie, instead of thanking you, how about I give your documentary a plug?

DANA GOLD

You help me with so many things that are hard for me to deal with. Simple tasks like writing emails, paying bills, and basic banking are excruciating for me, but because of you I don't have to think about them and can just concentrate on comedy. You make me breathe more easily on a daily basis. This is something I think about often but seldom tell you. You are very appreciated. Thank you.

DUNCAN STRAUSS

You were my first manager in L.A. You came to my shows and always had kind words for me afterwards. Your comments were especially meaningful because you covered stand-up for the *L.A. Times* and wrote about comedians I liked; when you became a manager and offered to sign me, I felt like I hit the lottery. You were everything I could want in a manager: diligent, smart, and sure of my ability to succeed. On top of all that, you were a decent person and that goes a long way. When you eventually decided to get out of managing, you made sure I found a new manager who would suit my needs. My career—past, present, and future—will always owe plenty to your guidance and support. So thanks . . . and say hi to Colleen and Mikey!

ALEX MURRAY

In this business, everybody wants their manager to think that they're funny and to genuinely believe in them. It sounds obvious, but it doesn't always happen, and even when it does, you're not always sure that it's real. With you, Alex, I'm always sure. You are everything anyone could ever want in a manager: supportive, gentle, and proud. You also gave me one of the best pieces of advice I got about coming out, reminding me that I just might have to do it before I was ready to. It's an insight that I will never forget. Thank you for all the love, support, and countless laughs. I love you. Thanks also to his assistants, Peter and Jerilyn—you aren't so bad yourselves!

MY TEACHERS

I want to thank every single teacher I had, kindergarten through twelfth grade, from the bottom of my heart. Even when you didn't know why I wasn't able to read, do math, or just concentrate, you never made me feel dumb for it. You always took the time to talk to me and made me feel genuinely listened to. You all will always have a special place in my heart.

DAN SAVAGE, TERRY MILLER, AND THE YOUTUBE KID

The It Gets Better campaign was started by Dan Savage and his partner, Terry Miller, to let kids know that, although they're struggling now, their lives are going to get easier. But I'm not sure they anticipated that it would help a full-grown man like me. The night before I went on WTF, I let my old fears get the best of me and began to have second thoughts. So I went online and looked at some It Gets Better videos. Seeing all these kids suffering needlessly reminded me that if my story could help any of them, I didn't have a choice. Eventually I came across a YouTube video of a thirteen-year-old kid coming out to the world in a self-taped confession. He was so smart, eloquent, and honest that I began to cry as he spoke. Here I was thinking that my coming out might help some kids, but somehow this kid on YouTube was helping me do it. The irony was not lost on me.

MR. ROGERS

As I get older and start to become aware of issues that I'm passionate about, I realize that these were things you were battling forty years ago. Every time I read something you said it makes me melt. I understand why people say that when they met you they were reminded of how good we can be as a species. I hope you're happy wherever you are. Thank you.

PHIL DONAHUE

When I was growing up, there were a lot of hot-button issues bubbling up for debate; racism, sexism, and homophobia were much more present in American society. Phil Donahue was the first adult I saw on TV discussing these issues in a manner that resonated with me. It was fun to watch the way he would talk to an audience of often intelligent but confused people, disarming their ignorant arguments without screaming or insulting them. The way he used questions to let people talk themselves out of certain opinions was absolutely brilliant. To me, Phil Donahue was a voice for anything that was different, but not wrong. He stood up for the disenfranchised when no one else did. I loved watching that show and if I ever meet him I'm going to give him a huge hug. Thank you, Phil, for helping me breathe more easily.

DR. DREW AND DR. PHIL

I find it admirable whenever somebody gives a voice to someone who doesn't have one—especially when those someones are children. Sometimes I'll watch your shows and see kids who, to the outer world, might seem angry and in need of discipline. The two of you always seem willing to dig a little deeper to find the source of the anger, linking it to hurt, sadness, or just not being heard. It's inspirational enough to make me break down and cry. I know there are other people out there doing the work you do, and I'm sure you would agree that we owe thanks to them, but I'm sending them your way (as well as to Dr. Phil's wife, Robin) because you're the ones I watch on my television every day.

DR. EBERT

Thank you, thank you, thank you. You're a good man, and my family is lucky to have you. If you live near Bala Cynwyd, Pennsylvania, and you need a good therapist, find him.

MARK AND WALT

You are special to me. Now you know. Thank you.

DANIEL GREENBERG

What can I say? None of this would have happened if it wasn't for you. Thank you. The end.

EVERYONE AT SIMON & SCHUSTER

I remember being very nervous about our meeting. I held on to this secret for so many years and now I had to walk into a roomful of strangers and talk about it? When you asked me if the book was autobiographical, I almost lied and said it was about a friend of mine. I was sweating so much someone actually had to go into another room and get a fan. But by the end of the meeting, I was completely dry. You guys could not have been easier to talk to. I remember telling my manager afterward that I really wanted you guys to tell my story. I was so happy that it worked out that way. That you also published George Carlin's autobiography is the cool icing on the cake. An extra-special thank you to Sarah Knight, who may have inherited the project but from the start treated us as one of her own. Thank you.

DANIEL KINNO

We laugh at the same stuff. Get upset at the same stuff. Get emotional at the same stuff. Cherish the same stuff. We were already great friends when, about a year ago, we started this book. It was overwhelming to me. I couldn't even imagine where to start. Getting me where I had to be took a lot of talking, a lot of patience, and a lot of nurturing. I don't know how I could have done this without you. This journey has brought us even closer—you certainly know more about the details of my life than anybody I know. I really value your friendship. Thank you for helping this all to happen.

ACKNOWLEDGMENTS

JONATHAN GROTENSTEIN

Even though this book tells my story the way I wanted it and it is in my voice on every single page, it took a lot of effort on your part to get it out of me and put it on paper. When you're a guy who's never read a book and barely graduated from high school (and by "barely" I mean "didn't"), "writing" means baring your soul to a complete stranger. Luckily, we didn't stay strangers for long. You're smart, funny, and easy to talk to, which made our time together not only productive but very enjoyable. Thank you for all your hard work.

WHERE ARE THEY NOW?

While writing this book, I really enjoyed reliving some of the fun moments of my childhood, especially as I talked to the people from back then who were most important to me. There were some people, however, who I would have loved to talk to but didn't know how to contact. So here are some of their names. My hope is that someone reading this might know them and can help me to reach out. Thanks!

Tom and Ileen Scott (From Philadelphia—last I heard they moved to Atlantic City in 1971.)

Nick and Francis D'Arco (They lived across on Joan Drive in Southampton in 1975. Daughter Meg was a nurse.)

Mrs. Zigler (My second-grade teacher at Davis Elementary School, 1972.)

Mrs. Biazzi (Teacher in the Resource Room at Davis Elementary School, 1972.)

Mr. Macolroy (Conestoga High School, 1982.)

ABOUT THE AUTHOR

TODD GLASS has been a professional stand-up comedian since he was sixteen. He could drop a bunch of names and list a bunch of credits, but how funny would that be? This is his first book.